TWAYNE'S WORLD AUTHORS SERIES

A Survey of the World's Literature

Sylvia E. Bowman, Indiana University

GENERAL EDITOR

CHINA

William R. Schultz

EDITOR

Ts'ao Yü

(TWAS 201)

TWAYNE'S WORLD AUTHORS SERIES (TWAS)

The purpose of TWAS is to survey the major writers —novelists, dramatists, historians, poets, philosophers, and critics—of the nations of the world. Among the national literatures covered are those of Australia, Canada, China, Eastern Europe, France, Germany, Greece, India, Italy, Japan, Latin America, the Netherlands, New Zealand, Poland, Russia, Scandinavia, Spain, and the African nations, as well as Hebrew, Yiddish, and Latin Classical literatures. This survey is complemented by Twayne's United States Authors Series and English Authors Series.

The intent of each volume in these series is to present a critical-analytical study of the works of the writer; to include biographical and historical material that may be necessary for understanding, appreciation, and critical appraisal of the writer; and to present all material in clear, concise English—but not to vitiate the scholarly content of the work by doing so.

Ts'ao Yü

By JOHN Y. H. HU
National Taiwan University

Twayne Publishers, Inc. :: New York

Printed in U.S.A. by
NOBLE OFFSET PRINTERS, INC.
New York, N.Y. 10003

DEDICATED TO
OSCAR G. BROCKETT

Preface

According to most literary historians,[1] Ts'ao Yü is the greatest writer of Chinese "spoken drama," a form introduced into China during the opening decade of the present century. His first play, *Thunderstorm* (1933), was the earliest modern Chinese play to achieve critical and commercial success; it still appeals to audiences in China, Russia, and the United States. His latest work, *The Gall and the Sword* (1961), written in compliance with Communist doctrine, has generally been praised by Communist critics as the best historical play on the subject. During the thirty years that separated these plays, Ts'ao Yü wrote seven other full-length plays; many of them won immediate success and remain powerful and interesting. Yet, despite this achievement Ts'ao Yü has never been the subject of a full-length critical study. The present work seeks to fill that lack by examining all of Ts'ao Yü's full-length plays and one of his short plays, *Just Thinking* (1940), which marks an important transition in his development as a playwright.

Born in 1910, Ts'ao Yü grew up and wrote in the most turbulent and exciting period in Chinese history. The monarchical government, the Confucian culture, the class structure, the large family system, all these and other political and social traditions which had continued for thousands of years were challenged, undermined, and finally swept away. On the other hand, a new China was being born amid problems of industrialization, new social injustices, and political strife. Since Ts'ao Yü's plays reflect many of these changes, they contribute much to an understanding of this drastically transitional period.

Ts'ao Yü's literary career is an odyssey in search of a Utopia. Starting as a bitter critic of the existing social and cultural systems, Ts'ao Yü gradually grew more temperate as he developed a tragic vision, though he continued to insist that the old systems must be replaced by better ones. Since Ts'ao Yü's works are so closely related to the socio-political events of his time, they have often been judged in terms of their ideology. On the one hand,

Communist literary historians praise him for his exposure and denunciation of the "old society" but disapprove of his "pseudo-humanitarianism" and nonrealistic dramatic techniques.[2] On the other hand, Nationalist critics condemn Ts'ao Yü's "subversive" messages and pro-Communist attitude.[3] Since most of Ts'ao Yü's major works are extremely popular, their protest and demand for reform have been widely discussed and should not be overlooked. Thus, the present study considers not only the socio-political implications of his works, but seeks to trace this ideological development as well.

In drama, however, considerations of ideology are inadequate at best. Unlike political pamphlets, which appeal primarily to the intellect and directly expound their author's opinions, dramatic works appeal to the emotions as well as to the intellect through a series of connected events, which must be explored and analyzed before adequate conclusions can be drawn about their meanings, effectiveness, or socio-political implications. Thus, in the present study, the dramatic incidents and their interrelations, the characters, the thought, the dialogue, and the setting will be examined. Understandably, a study of the present scope cannot exhaust all of these parts in each play, but each aspect will be considered whenever relevant.

This critical approach differs not only from the dogmatic, doctrinaire approach; it differs also from the comparative approach, which many recent critics writing in English have used in treating individual plays by Ts'ao Yü.[4] Obviously, the comparative studies have necessarily given some attention to the structure of Ts'ao Yü's plays, and the present study occasionally compares Ts'ao Yü to Sophocles, Shakespeare, O'Neill, Chekhov, Brecht, and other Western playwrights. The difference between the comparative approach and the one used here may be only a matter of degree, but it leads to interpretations which sometimes differ drastically. Since the judgments made in this work are based upon a careful analysis of the plays as artistic wholes quite apart from possible parallels with other works, however, the reader may verify for himself which interpretation is most firmly grounded in relevant evidence.

In the study which follows, each chapter is devoted to a particular play. The analysis of each play usually begins with a brief expository sketch concerning the circumstances surrounding the work's composition and its reception by the audience. In a few instances, this section is extended to provide some information about the action or the psychology of the characters so that the reader may better understand the discussion which follows. The script itself is then discussed in terms of the major lines of action, the means used to develop them, and their overall significance. In order to trace Ts'ao Yü's development as a dramatist, the chapters are arranged in the chronological order in which the plays were written. The concluding chapter will attempt to evaluate Ts'ao Yü's achievement as a playwright.

In addition to chapters devoted to individual plays, the Introduction traces the development of Chinese spoken drama and summarizes Ts'ao Yü's life and dramatic career. It shows how the Western mode was introduced into China and how it nurtured Ts'ao Yü's dramatic talent. Benefiting from material only recently made available, the Introduction, though brief, is probably the most detailed and up-to-date account of the subject in English.

I feel grateful to Professor Wu-chi Liu and Professor Walter Meserve, who have generously given me access to their personal collections and files as well as having saved me from making a number of factual errors. To Professor Richard L. Scammon, I owe a debt that extends beyond the academic aspect in the past years. Mr. James Fu has helped me with the romanizing of the Chinese characters; my wife Julie has borne more than the burden of typing and editing; she has also given me much needed hope and encouragement.

JOHN Y. H. HU

East Lansing, Michigan

Contents

Chronology

CHAPTER 1

Introduction

IN 1907 in Japan, Tseng Hsiao-k'u and other Chinese students there organized the Spring Willow Society and produced one act of *La Dame aux Camélias* by Dumas *fils*. Later in the same year, with such new members as Ou-yang Yü-ch'ien, the Spring Willow Society produced *A Negro Slave Supplicating Heaven for Succor*, a full-length play based on the Chinese translation of Mrs. Stowe's *Uncle Tom's Cabin*. After producing three one-act plays in 1908, they went on in the succeding year to present *Hot Blood*, another full-length work adapted from the Japanese translation of Sardou's *La Tosca*. A new phase in Chinese theater was thus initiated with these productions, even though the plays were based on foreign sources, the stages and scenery were rented from Japanese troupes, and the audiences were multinational.[1]

From the very beginning, the Western form of drama was used mainly as a vehicle for ideas. While Mrs. Stowe's *Uncle Tom's Cabin* is imbued with Christian devotion and humanism, its Chinese adaptation totally disregards the religious spirit and stresses the rebellion of the oppressed.[2] Similarly, in *La Tosca*, Baron Cavaradossi muses over the termination of his artistic career before being executed for his revolutionary ideas, but in *Hot Blood*, the Baron's last will and testament express his conviction that dictatorship will soon be overthrown and that a nation built on the principles of liberty and equality will finally prevail.[3] It was for the dissemination of such revolutionary messages that the Spring Willow Society was organized; it was to suppress such thought that Manchu magistrates in Japan threatened to cut off financial aid to students involved in further productions. Since all important members of the Society were recipients of government aid, the first phase of modern Chinese drama ended in 1909.

After the Manchu Dynasty was overthrown in 1911, most members of the Spring Willow Society returned to China and resumed production. Other troupes were also organized. For approximately three years, people came to the theater to get new ideas or to hear comments on current events in a way reminiscent of the early Elizabethan theater. Furthermore, the patriotic speeches, mostly concocted by the actors extemporaneously and delivered flamboyantly, thrilled the audiences. But, as these comments and speeches tended to be repetitive and the actors' dissipations became scandalous, attendance declined rapidly by 1914-15.

In the beginning, there was no special designation for this new approach. It was simply called "New Theater" and "New Drama" to distinguish it from traditional theater and drama. Later, its enthusiastic supporters called it "Civilized Drama" or "Modern Drama" in order to separate it from the indigenous drama, which they regarded as backward. In 1927, the playwright T'ien Han, recognizing that the new drama was essentially conversational and that the old drama was essentially operatic, used the designation "spoken drama" (hua-chü), which has since been generally accepted.[4]

The surge of New Chinese Literature that started in 1917 and reached a high tide in 1919 in the May Fourth Movement gave a new impetus to spoken drama. From then on, spoken drama steadily evolved into a major form of literature. The first play to achieve both critical and commercial success, however, was not to appear until Ts'ao Yü wrote *Thunderstorm* in 1933 (not produced until 1935).[5] Thus, the evolution in the theater between 1917 and 1933 deserves mention in a study on Ts'ao Yü not only because it paved the way for his success but also because it sheds light on his works.

Several factors help to clarify the path which spoken drama took. First, in 1918 the *New Youth Monthly* touched off a controversy concerning the function of theater. The majority argued that theater should be primarily a forum for instruction. In an article entitled "Ibsenism," Hu Shih advocated introducing Ibsen's works into China because Ibsen's sound individualism, as personified in Nora and Dr. Stockmann, demonstrates the kind of enlightened views towards which China should be moving. In 1921, the People's Dramatic Society declared, "Though Bernard Shaw is not necessarily right when he says that theatre is the place to propagate ideas, it is certainly true that the age when theatre-going is merely for entertainment is gone."[6] Other critics, such as P'u Po-ying, cited Gordon Craig, Romain Rolland, Upton Sinclair, and other Western critics to prove that theater should give "sugar-coated" instruction.[7]

Advocates of Art-for-Art's-Sake and other esthetic theories, although numerous, were outnumbered and overcome. Especially after 1930, when the League of Leftist Playwrights was founded, the predominant trend was towards an extremely militant socialist realism. During the early phase of the controversy over the theater's function, many critics challenged the social value of the traditional Chinese theater. Extremist reformers, such as Fu Ssu-nien, found in the traditional theater little more than superstition, injustice, and inhumanity.[8] Consequently, they advocated its abolition. Though Mei Lan-fang and other famous Peking Opera actors continued to enjoy great popularity, the younger generation tended to be inimical to the traditional theater and sympathetic to spoken drama.

The second important influence came through translations and adaptations of foreign plays. According to critic Cheng Chen-to, thirty-three plays were translated into Chinese between 1918 and 1921.[9] Incomplete statistics compiled in 1944 note that 387 translations of plays were published between 1908 and 1938.[10] Of the total, only six were published before 1920. The same sources also show that 132 were originally French; 127, English; eighty-four, Japanese; seventy, Russian; forty-three, American; forty-two, German; eighteen, Greek; and sixteen, Irish. Twenty of these plays were written by Shakespeare, fourteen by Chekhov, twelve each by Shaw and Galsworthy, and nine by Ibsen.

The third event of far-reaching consequences was Ch'en Ta-pei's advocacy of amateur theater. Attributing the rapid decline of spoken drama during the 1914-18 period partly to the selfishness of the managers who considered box office receipts paramount, Ch'en Ta-pei and his supporters encouraged the establishment of nonprofessional troupes.[11] Though amateurism in English implies less than perfection, its Chinese characters (Ai-mei; love-beauty) connote the original meaning of "amateur" as "a lover of." Amateur theater thus demands high esthetic standards but promises little material reward.

Related to this theory was the rapid multiplication of school and community dramatic troupes and the foundation of academies specializing in the training of theater artists. The People's Dramatic Society and the Shanghai Drama Association, both

founded in Shanghai in 1921, were followed the next year by the
South China Society in Canton. In 1922, P'u Po-ying, Ch'en
Ta-pei, and others organized the first school of spoken drama,
the Peking Jen-i Drama Academy. In 1925, the Peking Academy
of Fine Arts added a drama department. After these pioneering
events, school dramatic clubs, amateur and professional dramatic troupes mushroomed in large cities. These organizations
not only produced plays, they trained theater artists and provided opportunities for the younger generation to observe and
participate.

Another important advance during these fermenting years was
made in theater arts—in acting, directing, lighting, costume, and
makeup—and the integration of all these elements into a harmonious and unified whole. During the production of *A Negro
Slave Supplicating Heaven* in 1907, schoolmates of the major
actors—students from Japan, India, and Korea—impersonated
minor characters and appeared on stage in their colorful native
costumes.[12] In later years, complaints about the actors' lack of
discipline and the incompetence of other personnel recurred
often. But on the whole, spoken drama moved away from
naiveté and inexperience towards artistry and sophistication.

In addition to experiment and practice, improvement was made
by absorbing skills and methods from the world's advanced
theaters. After the foundation of the *Drama Monthly* in 1921,
books, magazines, and newspaper articles on theater arts became more plentiful. The Stanislavsky system of acting was introduced into China in 1937, thirteen years after his *My Life in Art*
was written.[13] Furthermore, a few students who had studied
theater abroad brought home their knowledge and experience.
Among them, Hung Shen deserves particular praise. A student
of George Pierce Baker, he acquired practical training in theater
in Workshop 47 at Harvard, in Dr. S. S. Curry's school, and in
the Crown Theatre in Boston.[14] After his return to China in
1922, he served as actor, playwright, director, and critic, as well
as in many other positions. Perhaps more importantly, he engi-
neered the abolition of male actors in female roles and elevated
the position and authority of the director.[15]

Considering the pragmatic functions for which the spoken
drama was promoted, all these improvements would have re-
mained ineffective if a native spoken drama had failed to develop,
for, even though translations and adaptations had been chosen

carefully, they never proved completely congenial to Chinese audiences. The production of *Mrs. Warren's Profession* in 1921, despite intense publicity and a fairly good performance, was a commercial fiasco.[16] A quarter of the audience left before the production was over, some of them using obscenities on their way out. This failure discouraged professional producers, hardened their doubts about foreign plays, and caused Ch'en Ta-pei and others to advocate "amateurism" in an effort to save spoken drama. Generally speaking, the social and cultural gaps between China and other countries at that time were so great that foreign plays had little chance of becoming popular. Consequently, a native spoken drama developed rapidly during the decade before Ts'ao Yü made his literary debut.

One group of these plays, such as Hsiung Fu-hsi's *Western Chuan-yüan* and *The Artist* and Ting Hsi-lin's *Oppression* and *The Hornet*, are lighthearted comedies or farces. Another group, such as Hsiang P'ei-liang's *Melancholy Plays* and T'ien Han's early works (including *Tragedy on the Lake*, *A Night at the Café*, and *The Death of a Famous Actor*), reflects the personal frustration and anguish of the young writers. Neither group was in the mainstream of spoken drama and T'ien Han, near the end of the 1920s, became a militantly leftist playwright.[17]

The majority of the early plays, however, are social problem plays which either deal directly with contemporary problems or reinterpret historical stories in order to demonstrate certain messages. In a comparatively serene tone, Hu Shih's *Life's Great Affair*, written originally in English and then translated into Chinese and published in 1919, tells the story of a girl who asserts her freedom in marriage. She tacitly resists the superstitious and irrational arguments against her marriage and, somewhat like Isben's Nora, leaves her parental home to seek her own happiness. Other playwrights, as a protest against parental control, usually chose to dramatize the anguish (and sometimes the pathetic deaths) resulting from arranged marriages. Yang Yin-sheng's *Rocks and Reeds*, Yüan Ch'ang-yin's *The Peacock Flies Southeast*, and another play with the same title (but written by the senior class of a girl's college) all depict the folktale of a young couple who commit suicide after having been separated by the husband's mother.

If submission to parental order implies unhappiness, as these plays obviously suggest, there are a number of other plays which

eulogize Cho Wen-chun and other women in history who openly
rebelled against social and domestic authorities in order to seek
personal fulfillment. The most famous of these plays are Kuo
Mo-jo's trilogy of *Three Revolutionary Women* (1923). "He
takes three famous women—Wang Chao-chun, Cho Wen-chun,
and Nieh Ying," a literary historian writes on Kuo Mo-jo, "from
Chinese history as his theme; he mercilessly attacks the moral
code of the old society under the guise of opposing the corrupt
feudal system."[18] In general, these early plays tend to show
either the triumph and happiness of the rebels or the pathetic
fate of the submissive. Ts'ao Yü, on the other hand, often
creates a synthesis by presenting in one play both outcomes.
This is one instance of the way in which Ts'ao Yü remains in the
mainstream of spoken drama while surpassing other playwrights.

Of the plays dealing with other contemporary social problems,
Hung Shen's *Yama Chiao* (1922), an anti-civil war tragedy, has
several scenes which use expressionistic techniques, like those
in *Emperor Jones,* to present aboriginal fear. The author admitted that he was moved to write the play by his sympathy
for the downtrodden peasant and the misused soldier. The name
Yama Chiao, the expressionistic techniques, and the sympathy
for the downtrodden were all to be used effectively by Ts'ao Yü
in *The Wild.*[19]

In view of the circumstances under which spoken drama
evolved, it is not surprising that its critics and playwrights used
it to propagate ideas conducive to the reform of a moribund
society and backward country. The humiliation that China had
suffered since the Opium War (1839-42), the chaotic political
situation following the collapse of the Manchu Dynasty, the
increasing conflicts between the Nationalists and Communists
during the 1920s and 1930s, the widespread corruption and injustice in society, the malaise in the traditional culture, and the
intensified Japanese aggression—all of these and other events
disturbed Chinese intellectuals. Thus, not only spoken drama,
but fiction and poetry as well, reflected the same anxieties and
preoccupations with social and political problems. In *Twentieth
Century Chinese Poetry: An Anthology*, Kai-yu Hsu writes:

The literary pioneers were understandably preoccupied with the
ugly physical reality in which they lived. The change of seasons,
the pain of parting, reminiscences of the past, and the serenity of

the natural universe were no longer the immediate subjects of the poet's concern. They had become too remote and irrelevant. It was the ricksha pullers laboring under a scorching sun, the tears of a child-bride married to a total stranger three times her age, the silent protest of an abused boy-apprentice, the misery of a peasant family unable to sell their homespun cloth for food that aroused sympathy in the new poet, Liu Ta-pai (1880-1932).[20]

Concerning modern Chinese fiction, C. T. Hsia has observed: "The reformist urge, which accounts for the shallow character of the early romanticism, inevitably leads to a patriotic didacticism. Perhaps even without the massive influence of Communist practice and ideology, the moral exploration of the mind would still remain an expendable luxury to most writers who, in their earnest effort to transform China into a modern nation, took upon themselves primarily the task of educating their benighted countrymen."[21]

Ts'ao Yü shares the poets' concern for the downtrodden and the novelists' ambition to reform the nation. Probably born in 1910 to a well-to-do family in Tientsin,[22] Ts'ao Yü, whose real name is Wan Chia-pao, received the best available formal education and practical theatrical experience. He attended Nankai Middle School in Tientsin where he was a member of the dramatic club between 1926 and 1930. During this time he acted in Ibsen's *An Enemy of the People* and other plays and co-translated Galsworthy's *Strife*. From 1931 to 1934, he studied English at the National Tsing Hua University in Peking, from which he received a B.A. degree.

During his junior year at the university, Ts'ao Yü wrote the epoch-making *Thunderstorm*. Concerning the actual process of composition, he recalled: "I was not clearly aware that I wanted to rectify, satirize, or attack anything. Near the end of the writing, however, there seemed to be an emotional surge pushing me forward, and I was releasing and transforming my suppressed anger into bitter denunciation of the Chinese family and society. But in the beginning, when I began to form a vague image of *Thunderstorm*, what interested me was a couple of episodes, a few characters, as well as a complex and aboriginal sentiment."[23]

From this beginning, Ts'ao Yü launched his dramatic career and his literary odyssey in search of a Utopia. *Thunderstorm* was published in the *Literary Quarterly* in 1934 and was produced in 1935 by students of Futan University under the direction of Hung Shen and Ou-yang Yü-ch'ien. In 1936, the Travelling Dramatic Troupe took the play on tour and achieved a critical and commercial success greater than that of any other modern Chinese play either before or since.

After his graduation from Tsing Hua, Ts'ao Yü taught at the Tientsin Normal College for Women for a short period before being appointed principal of the National Academy of Dramatic Arts in Nanking.[24] Tientsin, the largest seaport in North China, had all the evils of a commercial cosmopolitan city, and these were increased in 1933 by repercussions from the American stock market collapse. Nanking, the capital of the Republic of China, is only a few hours by train from Shanghai, a seaport much larger than Tientsin. Concerning his life during this period, Ts'ao Yü has vividly reminisced: "Drifting in the bizarre and stupendous society in recent years, I have seen nightmarishly terrible events, whose impressions will be indelible on my mind until my death. They, these serious problems, attack me at full force, inflaming my feelings, aggravating my complaint against injustice. Like a delirious man, I feel all day long the presence of a haunting ghost whispering demands to me, torturing me, and depriving me even of a momentary rest."[25]

On many dark nights Ts'ao Yü could endure the depression no longer. Of one of these nights he has written: "During the emotional outbursts, I broke many precious mementoes, including my most beloved porcelain statue of the Buddhist Goddess of Mercy, which my mother gave me as a charm and toy, when I was two years old. I groaned desperately, wishing for total annihilation. Like a wounded dog, I crawled on the ground, licked the piquant earth, and felt that the universe had shrunk into a dark ball, suffocating my breath. My hand, tightly grasping some dirt, felt wet and sticky. I lighted a match and was amazed to see blood; the porcelain fragments had cut a slash in my thumb and blood was dripping, drop by drop, soothingly."[26]

As with *Thunderstorm*, this anguish and indignation provided the basis for Ts'ao Yü's next two plays: *Sunrise* (1935), which attacks social injustice in a large city, and *The Wild* (1936), which features an oppressed peasant's revenge. *Sunrise* won the literary prize of the *Ta-kung Daily* as the best play of 1936, an honor comparable to the Pulitzer Prize in America.

In 1937, when Ts'ao Yü was teaching at his alma mater, the National Tsing Hua University, the Sino-Japanese War broke out. Before Nanking fell to the Japanese, the National Academy of Dramatic Arts was moved to Chungking; Ts'ao Yü was its principal for an unascertainable period. Despite heavy administrative duties while in office, and frequent lectures, Ts'ao Yü was very productive in these years. He finished three original plays—*Metamorphosis* (1940), *Peking Man* (1940), and *The Bridge* (1945), and completed two adaptations—*Family* (1941) from Pa Ch'in's novel of the same name, and *Just Thinking* (1940), based on *The Red Velvet Goat* by the Mexican playwright Josephina Niggli. In these years he also translated *Romeo and Juliet.*

After the founding of the Chinese Communist Party in 1921, the conflicts between the Communists and the Nationalists were incessant, even during wartime when nominal unity prevailed. Their contention in the ideological field involved a great number of prominent writers, but Ts'ao Yü maintained his independence in action as well as in thought. Immediately before and after the composition of his first two plays, a Communist literary historian writes: "The December 9 Movement of 1935, which was led by the Chinese Communist Party, broke out in Peking where he was studying but he hardly noticed it."[27] To *The Bridge* (1945), Ts'ao Yü prefixed a quotation from Milton: "Give me the liberty to know, to utter, and argue freely according to conscience, above all liberties."[28] As he matured, his early nihilistic and anarchic tendencies were replaced by a more mellow attitude toward life and society. He still believed in the necessity of spiritual and intellectual changes, but he was also able to see the weaknesses as well as the nobility of humanity. If his early plays are vigorous and sometimes adolescent, the plays written during wartime frequently show a serene maturity.

After the war, in 1946, the United States Department of State invited Ts'ao Yü and Lao She, a foremost novelist, to visit America, apparently in recognition of their literary achievements. In an article published during his visit, Ts'ao Yü wrote:

It should be the purpose of the Chinese theater, therefore, to reflect the life and thought patterns of the Chinese people in the tumultuous age of cultural reevaluation. Our New Theater must not be an echo nor an imitation of the Western stage. Ibsen is no longer an idol, nor are the other great Western masters. We are looking for true playwrights with vision and sincerity—outgrowths of Chinese soil— whose words will mirror the soul of our people.[29]

In 1947, at the invitation of the Wen-hua Film Company in Shanghai, Ts'ao Yü wrote and directed *Sunny Sky*. The story concerns a chivalrous lawyer successfully defending an orphanage against illicit underground forces. In discussing the theme of the film, Ts'ao Yü writes: "We must distinguish the right from the wrong and dedicate ourselves to honest works, unafraid of troubles or certain people's hatred."[30] These words, and the passage from Milton which prefixed *The Bridge*, perhaps best define Ta'so Yü's ideals during the pre-Communist era; they are rarely to be heard from him again.

Since the Communist takeover, Ts'ao Yü has held a great number of official and semi-official positions, such as Vice President of the Central Dramatic Institute (1949), member of the board of directors of the All-China Dramatic Association (1952), President of the Peking People's Artistic and Dramatic Institute (1956), and Deputy for Hupei to the National People's Congress (1954, 1958, 1964).[31] Ts'ao Yü joined the Chinese Communist Party in 1956, after having worked in the Huai River project, in the land reform campaign, and as part of a team for the reform of intellectuals in Peking.[32]

The price that Ts'ao Yü has paid for survival in Peking appears to be complete submission and resignation, a conclusion suggested by his own writings. In 1952, Ts'ao Yü confessed that his previous plays, because of his ignorance of the thought of Mao Tse-tung and the Communist doctrine, were quite vague in outlook and ineffective in their attack against vices of the old society.[33] This denial of his past achievement is constant, as revealed in the preface to the 1958 English translation of *Thunderstorm*, and a number of articles.[34] A typical statement appears in the preface to his selected works:

Thinking over the past I remember that when I was writing the play I did want to pose certain problems and provide their solutions. But I was from beginning to end dominated by strong emotion. I did not write in a thorough-going fashion and so failed to make known the real origins of the evils I described. The play *Sunrise*, for instance, is evidently a denunciation of the old semi-feudal, semi-colonial society. But in writing it I unwittingly allowed imperialism, the greatest of evils, to pass without a single blow. This made the play read like a grandiloquent indictment of the evils of urban society which thinking men liked to read in those days. Another thing, I laid great stress on the life of the henchmen of the reactionary ruling class—their licentiousness and cruelty. But I never wrote about serious revolutionaries, the positive force of society, about their life-and-death struggles waged against the enemy.[35]

Under the Communist rule, Ts'ao Yü has not only denied his own achievement, but he has also expressed his support and allegiance to the Communists. In 1954, for example, when the constitution of the People's Republic of China was drafted, Ts'ao Yü wrote: "We must not forget for a moment that only under the leadership of the Chinese Communist Party and Chairman Mao can such a constitutional draft be produced.... What makes me feel most proud and excited are articles 100-103, the section that stipulates citizens' obligations. It profoundly tells us that the glory of being a citizen of New China is the fulfillment of the sacred obligation of a Chinese citizen."[36] In 1958, after the leading Party magazines had decided to reduce by half their payment to contributors, Ts'ao Yü advocated complete abolition of royalties for playwrights, or at the least a reduction by two-thirds of the current scale.[37] The most telling example, however, is connected with the purge of Hu Feng, a Communist Party member and a prominent man of letters, who bluntly criticized the Communist literary hierarchy and, by implication, the literary policy of Mao Tse-tung.[38] In the whirlwind of denunciations of Hu Feng in 1955, apparently initiated by the literary hierarchy, Ts'ao Yü wrote a one-page article which includes two significant passages. The first is a quotation from a broadcast made by a literary critic in Taiwan:

"In all conscience, Mr. Hu Feng's accusations are reasonable. He has accused Ho Ch'i-fang of having threatened writers with three sticks and having forced them to choose material from among factory workers, farmers and soldiers.... That is to say, the writers are permitted to praise the victory and glory of revolution, not to touch upon its backwardness; they are permitted to write on factory workers, farmers and soldiers only; even within such a limit, to write on the glorious aspects of their thought and emotions, not on the dark aspects. If the writers choose to write anything else or of anybody else, they will be criticized for being unsteady or insufficient in their political stand. How succinctly and poignantly Mr. Hu Feng's words have manifested the sorrow and dejection of writers on the Chinese Mainland today."[39]

Ts'ao Yü justifies his inclusion of this rather long quotation by pointing out that Hu Feng is so degenerate that even the reactionary critics of Taiwan and the Voice of America quote him and support him during the purge. But Ts'ao Yü conspicuously neglects to refute the accusations of these commentators. In the second passage he speculates:

Perhaps Hu Feng is thinking at this very moment: "Why should I ever have made such a gross error that brought nationwide criticism of me? In the past, if I had been more shrewd, restrained, and dissembling, would I not have been spared these troubles?"[40]

Ts'ao Yü's speculation on Hu Feng might be equally well applied to himself: if the comment of the literary critic in Taiwan holds no particular appeal for him, why should he quote it at such length? Is he not perhaps being shrewd, and dissembling in order not to provoke the Communist literary hierarchy? Hu Feng's punishment entailed thought reform through labor; he eventually died from exhaustion and malnutrition. Ts'ao Yü's fate has been less disastrous, but his submission has greatly curtailed his literary output.

During the Communist era, Ts'ao Yü has written only two plays: *Bright Skies* (1954) and *The Gall and the Sword* (1961).[41] The first of these plays, the winner of the first prize at the 1956 National Modern Drama Festival, is designed to demonstrate that intellectuals must undergo thought reform under the guidance of the Communist Party;[42] yet, in a discussion of the finished work, Ts'ao Yü apologizes for his poor understanding of Communist ideology and requests that the All-China Writers' Association design and conduct a program to raise writers' ideological standard. Furthermore, in a revealing expression of gratitude, Ts'ao Yü acknowledges that, in the process of writing and revising the play, many Party leaders have helped him so unreservedly that "*Bright Skies* is a team work and I am but a member of the team."[43] By these two strokes, Ts'ao Yü minimizes his responsibility both for any political error and for literary mediocrity.

In 1958, in coordination with the "Great Leap Forward" announced earlier that year by the Communist Party, the All-

China Writers' Association drafted a program of thirty-two articles to promote a great leap forward in literature. As one member of a panel of writers discussing these articles, Ts'ao Yü declared his support in a hyperbolic manner. He observed that the time for a rich harvest in literature was ripe, that only a catalytic stimulus was needed, and that the thirty-two articles would provide it. As if this demonstration of loyalty was still insufficient, he continued: "We must speed up our self-reform and create glorious works so as to greet the new crest in our literature."[44]

As far back as 1942, at the Yenan Forum on Art and Literature, Mao Tse-tung had laid down the stringent policy that would govern arts and letters under his rule. "The Party's artistic and literary activity," he decreed, "is subordinate to the prescribed revolutionary task of the Party in a given revolutionary period."[45] The prescribed task during the Great Leap Forward was to increase agricultural and industrial production at an ambitious and unattainable rate. Furthermore, since Soviet Russia was withholding its economic and technical assistance following a feud, Peking had to rely on its own resources for attaining the envisioned goal. Thus, hundreds of historical plays were written during this period to demonstrate that China in the past had overcome national ordeals and achieved great success. Ts'ao Yü's *The Gall and the Sword,* published in 1961, serves just such a purpose.

Both *Bright Skies* and *The Gall and the Sword* are thus, in all probability, involuntary productions. Both plays, however, reflect the political atmosphere in which they were written and, in a certain sense, continue Ts'ao Yü's efforts in his pre-Communist plays at building a strong and prosperous nation. In a discussion of Kuo Mo-jo, poet, playwright, and the president of the All-China Writers' Association, C. T. Hsia writes: "Properly understood, his career only underscores the more dramatically the tragedy of a generation of intellectuals who began in romantic revolt and ended in subservience to a despotism which they themselves had helped to create."[46] The same can be said of Ts'ao Yü.

Unlike Kuo Mo-jo, Ts'ao Yü did not join the Communist Party until 1956. His pre-Communist plays are the voluntary acts of a sensitive conscience and thus reflect the sincere desire for reform of a nonpartisan intellectual. While most other Chi-

nese playwrights' works have been forgotten, Ts'ao Yü's plays
are often produced in and outside China. Thus, it is most likely
that his major works will survive the test of time and remain
representative of a special genre in Chinese literature, one born
of foreign influences and growing to maturity in a traumatic-
ally transitional period.

With this background in mind, it is now possible to examine
Ts'ao Yü's development as a playwright from 1933 to 1961
through a chronological study of his work.

CHAPTER 2

Thunderstorm

SINCE Chou P'ing, son of P'u-yüan and Shih-p'ing, is planning to leave his wealthy but dreary family, his stepmother and former mistress, Fan-i, asks to be taken along. When refused, Fan-i threatens revenge.

During her visit to her daughter, Ssu-feng, who has been working in the Chou family as a maid, Shih-p'ing is surprised to discover that her daughter's employer is the man who seduced and abandoned her nearly thirty years ago. She decides to take her daughter away with her to the remote place whence she has just returned. On the eve of her departure, Ssu-feng meets Chou P'ing clandestinely in her bedroom. The jealous Fan-i blocks the exit of her estranged lover and thus exposes his illicit affair. Chou P'ing subsequently proposes to marry Ssu-feng, but Shih-p'ing adamantly refuses until she learns that her daughter has already become pregnant by her son.

Meanwhile, Chou P'u-yüan, in order to redeem himself and amend his errors, admits his former relationship with Shih-p'ing, thus inadvertently revealing the blood relationship of the young lovers. Guilt-stricken, Ssu-feng and P'ing commit suicide. In an attempt to save Ssu-feng, Fan-i's innocent son, Chou Ch'ung, is electrocuted. The Prologue and Epilogue to the play proper reveal that Shih-p'ing and Fan-i become insane as a result of the tragic events, while P'u-yüan is worn out by the sorrow of bereavement and loneliness.

Since its first production in 1935, *Thunderstorm* has been the most popular modern Chinese play. As late as 1961-62, a visitor seeing a production of *Thunderstorm* in Peking was told that *Thunderstorm* and *Sunrise* (Ts'ao Yü's second play) are invariably presented during the slow season, for they can assure full houses even when attendance at other plays is slack.[1] In Soviet Russia, sixty-five resident theater companies had decided by 1960 to retain *Thunderstorm* in their repertories; among

29

Chinese plays, only *Romance of the Western Chamber*, written
by Wang Shih-fu during the thirteenth century, can match
Thunderstorm's popularity in Russia.[2] In the United States,
where interest in modern Chinese theater is only recent,
Thunderstorm is one of the few plays that have been staged.
In view of such enduring and widespread popularity, *Thunderstorm* is indeed unique in the modern Chinese theater.

A brief look at some of its constituent elements will reveal
why it has enjoyed such sustained success. In the *Poetics*,
Aristotle stated that the theoretically best kind of tragedy
presents deeds such as "murder or the like" among members
of the same family;[3] that "such incidents have the very greatest
effect on the mind when they occur unexpectedly and at the
same time in consequence of one another";[4] that "the most
powerful elements of attraction in Tragedy" are "the Peripeties
and Discoveries";[5] and that "the best of all Discoveries ... is
that arising from the incidents themselves."[6] *Thunderstorm*
possesses each of these marks of tragedy, as well as a compact
and interesting structure.

Like *Œdipus* or *Ghosts*, *Thunderstorm* has a late point of
attack, and past events are recalled mainly to clarify or solve
immediate problems. Thus, the time of the events in the dramatic
action moves simultaneously backward and forward. The backward movement starts with the revelation of the love affair between Chou P'ing and Ssu-feng (one that began several months
ago) and terminates with the exposure of the love affair between
Chou P'u-yüan and Shih-p'ing nearly thirty years ago. This
last discovery changes the seemingly normal love relationship
of Chou P'ing and Ssu-feng into incest. Unable to bear the
stigma, they commit suicide and cause the death of the innocent
Chou Ch'ung, Chou P'ing's half-brother, when he attempts
to save Ssu-feng from being electrocuted.

The forward movement results from the efforts of practically
all the characters to improve their fortunes or the fortunes of
their loved ones. Yet their efforts serve only to entangle their
relationships until the dreadful past is fully exposed. Under-
lying this movement are implications that human beings are
extremely vulnerable and that even the best of intentions may
turn into instruments for one's own destruction.

The particular chain of events depends to a large extent on
coincidence—both mother and daughter have an identical ex-

perience, one generation apart, of entering into a love affair
and becoming pregnant by a young man of the same household.
In other words, the reversal depends on the revelation that
what has happened to Chou P'u-yüan and Shih-p'ing thirty years
ago is now being repeated by their children. Though such a
coincidence is rare in real life, the situation need not strain
dramatic probability if the dramatist treats it properly. The
following discussion will treat the human passions, the complicated human relationships, and their ramifications in such
a human situation, and how the playwright has handled them
in order to create a probable dramatic action.

The initial error has occurred nearly thirty years before the
play begins. At that time, Chou P'u-yüan, in order to seek a
more suitable match, ruthlessly drove from his house Shih-p'ing,
the maid who had borne him two sons, P'ing and Ta-hai. He
kept P'ing, passing him off as the son of his deceased wife, but
forced Shih-p'ing to take Ta-hai with her. Years later, Chou P'u-
yüan married Fan-i, whose good education and family background made the match seemingly suitable. Three years later,
in an unguarded moment, he disclosed his amatory relationship
with Shih-p'ing and incurred Fan-i's contempt and hatred.
Furthermore, his pursuit of success has resulted in recurrent and
prolonged absences from home. Even at home, as is shown in his
first appearance near the end of Act One, he is authoritarian
and dictatorial, as is often the case with a patriarch of a
traditional Chinese family. In proportion to his negligence and
insolence, domestic discontent and defiance have grown (although not openly) until a cataclysm seems inevitable. Neglected
and often humiliated by her husband, Fan-i has sought fulfillment and revenge by entering into an incestuous relationship
with her stepson, Chou P'ing, who, in turn, guilt-stricken and
frustrated, has seduced Ssu-feng without knowing that she is
his half-sister. Thus, because of Chou P'u-yüan's faults, a set
of extremely complicated and abnormal human relationships
has developed.

Despite this highly explosive background, the opening of
Thunderstorm is full of false hopes. On that sultry summer
morning, in order to reclaim her daughter (Ssu-feng), Shih-p'ing
is returning from work in a remote town. Meanwhile, Chou
P'ing is planning to leave home and start his career at his
father's mine, also far away. Although this arrival and departure

show the possibility of ending the incestuous relationships, they actually only serve to break the outward equilibrium and to precipitate a chain of actions and reactions which finally ruins the prosperous Chou family. The dramatic structure thus embodies the idea that men are not the architects of their own fates.

Inscrutable and surprising as the reversal of fortune is, every complication in the development seems inevitable in view of the complex human relationships which are largely summed up in the two triangular love affairs: that of Chou P'u-yüan with his wife Fan-i and his former mistress Shih-p'ing; and that of Chou P'ing with his stepmother (Fan-i) and the maid (Ssu-feng). These relationships have been formed prior to the opening of the play and will not be fully revealed till near the dénouement.

Involved in both love triangles, Fan-i, Chou P'u-yüan's embittered wife and his son's estranged mistress, is the chief engineer of the catastrophe. To save her strained relationship with Chou P'ing, Fan-i has summoned Shih-p'ing to take her daughter away so that the triangular love situation will end. But the pending departure makes Ssu-feng and P'ing realize that they really love and need each other. Fan-i begs P'ing to take her with him. She tries to arouse his sympathy for her as an ill-used and forlorn wife, but her plea falls on deaf ears. Desperate and angry, she recalls his oaths of immutable love made in moments of passion, but Chou P'ing is disgusted by her reminder of a past that he wants to forget. After all these conciliatory efforts have failed, Fan-i warns Chou P'ing that she will not bear being wronged by two generations of Chous. Resolved to desert her, P'ing answers stoically: "I have already taken that into account."[7] Since it is a hot, suffocating summer afternoon, Fan-i dismisses Chou P'ing with an ominous and symbolic remark: "All right, go then! But look out, now, the storm is going to come" (III, 530). Like Medea, Fan-i vacillates between extreme love and extreme hate. The turning point occurs in the following exchange, which recalls a passion long since cooled:

CHOU FAN-I: You have forgotten what you once said with a sigh in this room at midnight, when I was crying? You said you hated your father. You said . . . that you were ready to see your wish realized even if you had to commit parricide.

CHOU P'ING: You have forgotten that I was young then and it was the mad heat in me that made me utter such absurd words.

CHOU FAN-I: You have forgotten that though I was a few years older than you, I was after all your stepmother. Didn't you know that you shouldn't have spoken such words to me?

CHOU P'ING: Ah! (*Sighs*) The House of Chou had plenty of ancestors who did evil things and committed murder. At any rate, you shouldn't have married into the House of Chou where the air is saturated with sin.

CHOU FAN-I: Sin! Yes, exactly, sin. Your ancestors were never clean-handed and your house has always been dirty.

CHOU P'ING: You wouldn't pardon a young man who has committed a blunder as a result of a moment's muddleheadedness? (*Painfully knits his brow.*)

CHOU FAN-I: It is not a question of pardon or no pardon. At that time I had my coffin ready, peacefully and quietly awaiting my death. Then you came along and coaxed me to live again, but later you ignored me and left me to wither and thirst to death. Now you speak, what shall I do?

CHOU P'ING: That . . . that I don't know. What do *you* say?

CHOU FAN-I (*Emphatically, word by word*): I hope you will not go.

CHOU P'ING: What? You want me to keep you company in a house like this, to brood over my past sins, and to be suffocated to death like this?

CHOU FAN-I: Since you know that a house like this is capable of suffocating one to death, how could you go away alone and leave me here?

CHOU P'ING: You have no right to talk like this. You are the mother of brother Ch'ung.

CHOU FAN-I: No, I am not! I am not! Since I entrusted to you my life and reputation, I have paid no heed to anything else. I am not his mother. No, no, I am not even Chou P'u-yüan's wife.

CHOU P'ING (*Coldly*): Even if you don't recognize yourself as my father's wife, I still recognize myself as my father's son.

CHOU FAN-I (*Dumbfounded, as she didn't expect such a reply from Chou P'ing*): Ah! You are your father's son. You haven't come to see me these months, particularly because you are afraid of your father?   (III, 495-96)

"I still recognize myself as my father's son." Of all the reasons Chou P'ing could give to excuse himself, this is the most unkind, for in it he exalts the man most despised and hated by Fan-i and shows that his conscience is reviving. Trying to extricate himself from an immoral liaison, he invokes a morality that he has wantonly trespassed. Though his effort at reform is assuredly praiseworthy, to his partner in sin his reversal constitutes a betrayal. Although P'ing is pitiable and deserves forgiveness to a large extent, Fan-i, as she has desperately explained, cannot afford the luxury of pity. Her response, however, is made in ignorance of the intricate human relations in the family. Later, when her vengeance has exposed these relations and caused irreparable suffering, her own humanity will emerge and prevail. But, at this moment, she is concerned only with destroying the man who, in her opinion, has seduced and abandoned her. She has already sent for Ssu-feng's mother, whose arrival is vital to the development of the dramatic action.

Since Chou P'u-yüan abandoned her thirty years ago, Shih-p'ing has attempted suicide, has married and been widowed, and then remarried to Lu-kuei, a greedy and callous servant in the Chou house and father of her daughter, Ssu-feng. In order to help support the family, she left home some years ago to take a servant's position in a remote school where, because of her industry and honesty, she has won the trust of her employers. Before leaving home, Shih-p'ing, remembering her youthful transgression, has repeatedly warned her husband not to let Ssu-feng work in any household. Lu-kuei, however, has not heeded her advice.

Because she could not bring herself to confess her past, Shih-p'ing did not offer adequate reasons to explain her warnings. Her daughter has failed on her part to resist the physical temptation to which her mother once succumbed. Thus, when Shih-p'ing returns, Ssu-feng is pregnant by P'ing. On the surface, the error of the older generation is merely being repeated, but later when P'ing proves to be the son of Shih-p'ing, the terrible nature of the offense becomes evident. The sin of Chou P'u-yüan, the ultimate cause of these complications, unexposed and unexpiated for nearly thirty years and now repeated by his son, will finally exact an exorbitant price. As events of the past converge with those of the present, the action becomes increasingly suspenseful.

When Shih-p'ing enters the Chou house, the past and the present are practically linked; and when she realizes who the masters of her daughter really are, she is filled with fear and dread. She gradually recognizes the owner's identity because of the articles in the house.

Despite numerous moves which have taken the Chous from Southern to Northern China, P'u-yüan has preserved Shih-p'ing's favorite pieces of furniture, has kept her picture on his writing table, and has retained some of her peculiar habits, such as having the windows closed even on a hot summer day. When these signs make her realize in whose house she is, she cries: "Could this be true? This photograph, this furniture, how could they—? Oh, the world is so vast, and yet after these decades of suffering it should happen that this pitiful child of mine again falls into his—his house" (III, 506). The years, however, have changed Shih-p'ing's appearance so much that she has to show Chou P'u-yüan her knowledge about certain secrets which only they share to convince him that she is his abandoned mistress, reportedly dead for thirty years. If he had welcomed her eagerly at that moment, subsequent events would have been quite different. But such a response is impossible for Chou P'u-yüan. An analysis of his motivation for having kept Shih-ping's possessions will reveal that he is as eccentric now as he was thirty years ago.

As long as he was assured of her death and thus of his security, P'u-yüan could afford to indulge in nostalgia and to honor her memory by conveniently referring to her as his late first wife. Yet, in driving her out of the house with her newborn baby, Ta-hai, unprovided for, he incurred a stain on his character, which he might hide from society but not from himself. Thus, he needed some tangible signs which would restore his self-esteem as well as assure him of his humanity. Consequently, the ritualistic gestures of keeping her furniture are not altruistic deeds in honor of the deceased, but self-reassurances. Thus, when Shih-p'ing suddenly appears before him, shattering his sense of security, he immediately suspects blackmail. To buy her silence, he disregards her protests and writes her a check for five thousand dollars, which she immediately tears to pieces. Always resorting to expediency, he cannot comprehend the meaning of her protest; nor can he recognize the dignity that she has acquired through suffering during the intervening years.

Informed by Fan-i that her son, Chou Ch'ung, is very fond of Ssu-feng, Shih-p'ing decides to return to her school with her daughter the next day. With this decision and Ssu-feng's promise never to see any member of the Chou family again, there is a

ray of hope that tragedy may be averted. For though the incest
has already taken place, there is no immediate danger of its
exposure with the consequent qualms and deaths. But Shih-
p'ing's effort is thwarted, for as night falls, passion once more
overcomes the young lovers.

That night, worried that he may never see Ssu-feng again,
Chou P'ing enters her bedroom through the window. Like a
vengeful Fury, Fan-i secretly follows her estranged lover and
locks the window from the outside. Since the window is the
only retreat, a fact made clear through the setting and dialogue,
it is only a matter of time before Chou P'ing is found in a
compromising and explosive situation. Through stage lighting
and spectacle alone, Ts'ao Yü presents an unforgettable picture
of a betrayed woman's revenge:

The rumbling of thunder and the beating of the downpour; the
stage grows dim. A gust of wind tears the window open. Outside
is complete darkness. Suddenly a steel-blue flash of lightning shows
Chou Fan-i's pallid death-like face over the windowsill. Like a
corpse she lets the threads of rain lash her disheveled hair. She
laughs convulsively, but bitterly and softly, with tears draining
from the corners of her eyes, and stares at the cowering inmates
in the room. When the lightning flash ceases, darkness again reigns
in the space outside the window. When it flashes again she is seen
thrusting in her hands slowly to close the window.   (IV, 93)

In the sequel to the exposure of the tryst between her
children, Shih-p'ing evinces her boundless maternal love and
wisdom in protecting them. Knowing their true relationship, of
which they are ignorant, she persists in demanding their
immediate and permanent separation. Rejecting her mother's
pleas, Ssu-feng finally reveals her pregnancy. In the wake of
such a discovery, Shih-p'ing no longer sees any point in separat-
ing them, for the worst that can result from their association
has already occurred. Upholders of conventional morality
may argue plausibly for punitive measures or at least for an
immediate discontinuation of the relationship. But Shih-p'ing
blesses their intended marriage and wishes them happiness
thereafter. She knows that she is condoning an incestuous
marriage but, for the happiness of her children, she is willing
to keep silent. As she says: "They are my clean children and
they deserve to live in well-being and enjoy happiness. The

sin is in my heart and the punishment for it should also be suffered by me alone" (IV, 207).

Shih-p'ing thus far has endeavored to disentangle the second love triangle and, after she has failed, to conceal the first one. But her efforts are thwarted by Fan-i, who has been eavesdropping and now enters to stop the group from leaving the room. As her son has shown some affection for Ssu-feng, Fan-i urges him to make a scene and spoil P'ing's marriage, but Ch'ung merely says that if Ssu-feng has made her choice, he bears no grudge against her. Infuriated by her son's open-mindedness, Fan-i calls out for P'u-yüan:

CHOU P'ING (*To Chou Fan-i*): What does that mean?

CHOU FAN-I (*Coldly*): I want your father to see his future good children before you go. (*Calls*) P'u-yüan, P'u-yüan!

CHOU CH'UNG: Ma, please don't!

CHOU P'ING (*Goes to Chou Fan-i*): Lunatic, dare you shout again! (*Chou Fan-i runs to the study door and calls again.*)

LU SHIH-P'ING (*Getting anxious*): Ssu-feng, let's leave.

CHOU FAN-I: No, he has already come! (*Chou P'u-yüan enters from his study. Everyone is motionless and dead silent.*)

CHOU P'U-YÜAN (*At the door*): What are you calling me for? Why haven't you gone upstairs to sleep yet?

CHOU FAN-I (*Haughtily*): I am inviting you to meet your good relatives.

CHOU P'U-YÜAN (*Sees that Lu and Ssu-feng are also there and is astonished*): Ah, you—you—what are you doing here?

CHOU FAN-I (*Drags Ssu-feng*): This is your daughter-in-law, please meet her. (*To Ssu-feng—points at Chou P'u-yüan*) Call him your father! (*To Chou P'u-yüan, pointing at Lu*) Please also make the acquaintance of this old lady.

LU SHIH-P'ING: Mistress!

CHOU FAN-I (*To Chou P'ing*): P'ing, come here! Come here in the presence of your father, and *k'o-t'ou* to your mother-in-law.

CHOU P'ING (*Embarrassed*): Father, I—I—

CHOU P'U-YÜAN (*With full realization*): What—(*To Lu*) Shih-p'ing, so, after all, you have come back.

CHOU FAN-I (*Astonished*): What?

LU SHIH-P'ING (*Anxiously*): No, no, you are mistaken.

CHOU P'U-YÜAN (*In repentance*): Shih-p'ing, I thought that you would come back.

LU SHIH-P'ING: No, no! (*Droops her head*) Oh, Heaven!

CHOU FAN-I (*Overwhelmed with surprise*): Shih-p'ing? What? Is she Shih-p'ing?

CHOU P'U-YÜAN: Yes. (*With disgust*) Fan-i, you needn't purposely ask me. She is P'ing-erh's [the "erh" suffix means son] mother, who is supposed to have died thirty years ago.

CHOU FAN-I: Heavens!

An awkward suspense. Ssu-feng bursts out with a painful cry and stares at her mother, who is hanging her head down in suffering. Mentally confused, Chou P'ing looks in bewilderment at his father and Lu. Meanwhile, Chou Fan-i slowly moves to Chou Ch'ung. Now she has suddenly discovered a tragedy which makes her turn sympathetic towards Chou P'ing. She has come to realize her own madness of a moment ago, and this restores her normal maternal feelings. She looks shamefacedly in spite of herself at her own Ch'ung-erh.

CHOU P'U-YÜAN (*Overwhelmed with pain*): P'ing-erh, come here. Your mother is not dead, she is still living.

CHOU P'ING (*Half-insane*): It isn't she! Father, tell me that it isn't she!

CHOU P'U-YÜAN (*Sternly*): Silly fool! Don't talk nonsense, P'ing-erh. Though she has not had a decent life, she is still your mother.

CHOU P'ING (*Extremely pained*): Oh, Father!

CHOU P'U-YÜAN: If you should think that your "face" won't look nice because you have the same mother as Ssu-feng, then you have forgotten about family relations and human nature.   (IV, 213-14)

This is one of the best constructed scenes of recognition and reversal in dramatic literature and can be compared with the scene in which Œdipus discovers his true identity. Like Jocasta, Shih-p'ing attempts to prevent the revelation of the complex and incestuous relationship in the household. But from wrong reasoning, Œdipus and P'u-yüan insist on having their own way. Œdipus says of Jocasta: "Perhaps she is ashamed of my low birth, for she has all a woman's high-flown pride." Likewise, P'u-yüan tells P'ing: "She may not be from a good family, but she is your mother just the same." In maintaining that a humble birth should not deter one from admitting one's true identity, Œdipus and P'u-yüan alike attach more value to humanity and truth than ostensible class and rank.

This humanitarian trait, for Œdipus, is merely an extension of the ethical nature which has characterized his incessant search for Laius' murderer, but, for P'u-yüan, it marks a new turn in his character development. For thirty years, P'u-yüan has tried to evade responsibility for his youthful transgressions: he has abrogated his socio-familial duty by driving Shih-p'ing

and her newborn son away unprovided for; he has soothed his
guilty conscience by ritualistically preserving her possessions.
But Shih-p'ing's sudden return reveals to him that the woman
who could blackmail him is still alive. More seriously, when
he now drives her out and forbids her return to his house,
he proves to himself that he is selfish and hypocritical. The old
reassurances now become ineffective, and a willingness to
accept moral principles begins to grow; a new serenity, mingled
with a shade of resignation, permeates the subsequent action.
Thus, after having revealed Shih-p'ing's true relationship with
him, P'u-yüan says to his son:

P'ing-erh, please pardon me. All my life, I have only committed this
one blunder. I never suspected to this day that she was still living
and that she would find her way to this place. I think I can only
say that this is the will of Heaven. (*Sighs: to Lu [Shih-p'ing]*) I have
grown old. I regret very much that I told you to leave, and I had
planned to send you twenty thousand dollars. Now that you have
come, I think P'ing-erh is a pious child and he will certainly take
good care of you. He will make reparation to you for what I have
felt sorry for. (IV, 214)

This revelation proves to be more than Ssu-feng and Chou
P'ing can bear. Ssu-feng runs toward the garden where a high
voltage wire has not been repaired because of the intervening
thunderstorm. Fan-i, now regretting her revenge, sends her
son after Ssu-feng. This deep concern for the welfare of her
former archrival, like P'u-yüan's concern for the welfare of
Shih-p'ing, marks a new turn in her character development.
Thus, the older characters, the constituents of the first love
triangle, have demonstrated their good intentions: Shih-p'ing,
in order to secure the happiness of her children, has condoned
an incestuous marriage and assumed all the guilt herself;
P'u-yüan has admitted his error and offered to make amends;
and Fan-i has relented. But the situation is so intricate that
the efforts and best intentions of these characters only make
things worse. Ssu-feng is electrocuted and, in trying to help
her, so is Chou Ch'ung. Now anxious to preserve his last remaining son, P'u-yüan asks frenziedly that Chou P'ing be
brought back to him, but a pistol shot from the study signals
P'ing's suicide. The younger generation, except Ta-hai who
has never been close to P'u-yüan and will not be heard of again,

is totally wiped out. The resolution of *Thunderstorm* thus recalls that of *Romeo and Juliet,* in which the innocent die young, leaving their desolated parents to repent in their old age.

Without the complicated and partially concealed inter-personal relationships, the conflicts arising from the diverse motivations of the characters would not be so devastating. Without the traditional Chinese family system, in which the grown-up children still live with their parents, the incestuous relationship between Fan-i and P'ing would not have happened. But, in the final analysis, Chou P'u-yüan is more responsible than any other character for the tragic events, not only because it was he who made the initial false step, but also because, in order to preserve his reputation, it is he who has concealed the intricate human relationships. For his business gain, his social prestige, and his dignity at home, Chou P'u-yüan, until near the end of the play, is ready to forgo any moral principle and to sacrifice any other person. By exposing fully the selfishness and hypocrisy of Chou P'u-yüan, the patriarch of a traditional Chinese family and a pillar of Chinese society, *Thunderstorm* inevitably contains a disparaging evaluation of such family and social systems.

Ts'ao Yü has stated that near the end of writing the play, there seemed to be "a flow of surging emotion overwhelming me, I was venting a suppressed fury, defaming the Chinese family and society" (III, 272). Compared with Ts'ao Yü's later studies of the Chinese family system, *Peking Man* and *Family,* *Thunderstorm* is neither systematic nor penetrating. As a study of the uncertainty of human destiny, however, *Thunderstorm* occupies a unique position in Ts'ao Yü's dramatic works and has universal appeal.

This uncertainty of human fate is closely related to the inadequacy of human reason for controlling human passions and for coping with complex circumstances. The final efforts, by which the older generation attempts to avert the impending catastrophe, suggest that even well-intentioned action, because of inadequate knowledge about a complex situation, can hasten and magnify a catastrophe. The unfolding of this complex situation, so unpredictable and yet so inexorable, indicates, as the playwright himself has said, the existence of an oper-ational force in the universe which the Hebrews called God, the Greeks called Fate, and modern men name natural law.

The death of Chou Ch'ung, an innocent and kind adolescent, shows the indiscriminate cruelty of such a force.

Were human guilt and human passion absent, however, such an unknowable force might operate differently. In this way, then, the force is punitive, for it does not act unless it has been offended. The lamentation of Shih-p'ing, after having learned of the incest between her children, fully illustrates her understanding of this force:

Now I see, I see: it is already done, and it useless to resent unjust Heaven. Once a man sins, a second sin will naturally follow him.
(IV, 207)

Chou P'u-yüan's lamentation, upon the discovery that Shih-p'ing is still alive, provides another clue to the nature of this force:

P'ing-erh, please pardon me. All my life I have only committed this one blunder. I never suspected to this day that she was still living and that she would find her way to this place. I think I can only say that this is the will of Heaven.

Though this force is not personified into Fate, nor is its operation anticipated early in the play, the concept embodied in these lamentations approximates Sophocles' conception of *dike*, as explained by H. D. F. Kitto:

We will assume—in order to see what happens—that in the Electra *dike* means "the proper and natural order of things" not now in the physical universe, but in human affairs, moral and social. If the proper order is disturbed by some violence (*adikia*), it must, in the nature of things, restore itself, somehow; the restoration of the balance is an act of dike because it re-establishes dike. If so, we need not expect the act of dike to be agreeable in itself; the deluge that ends a drought may itself do harm.[8]

In their lamentations, both P'u-yüan and Shih-p'ing regret "the first misstep" or "the only real mistake" made years ago and they attempt to make amends. The recognition of an unknowable force thus tends to fill them with fear and urges them to propitiate it. But the fearsome nature of this force is fully revealed, not in the recognition of it by the sinners, but in the severe punishment inflicted on them. Disagreeable as this force is, as Kitto has said of *dike*, it is still just; yet, the sacrifice of so many young lives for the expiation of their parents' sin cannot fail to arouse pity and fear.

Apparently uncertain of the affective powers of the play, Ts'ao Yü surrounds the major incidents with a Prologue and an Epilogue. His expressed purposes for using this frame are to create esthetic distance lest the audience be unduly disturbed, and to introduce new characters who can function like a Greek chorus and end the play on a calm note. Set in the Chou house, now converted into a church-affiliated hospital, the action of the Prologue and Epilogue is supposed to take place ten years after the main action has concluded. While organ music plays in the background ("preferably Bach's Mass in B Minor"), Chou P'u-yüan, now wrinkled and melancholy, arrives to visit his wife and mistress who are now insane as a result of the tragic events of ten years ago. The nurses inform Chou P'u-yüan that his relatives have made little improvement and that Fan-i, in particular, has occasionally broken windows in her frenzies. When P'u-yüan goes to see his wife, Shih-p'ing comes in and peeps out the window for her only surviving child, Ta-hai, who has not been heard of in the past ten years. Disappointed once more, she finally kneels as if praying till the end of the Epilogue.

In addition, two characters, a fifteen-year-old girl and her younger brother who visit the hospital with their mother, serve as curious spectators. Thematically, however, their innocence and loveliness provide a perspective against which the guilt and bereavement of the Chous appear more dreadful and pathetic. Once the major characters must have been as innocent as these two youngsters now are, but the major body of incidents has shown how human passion overwhelms human reason and how inadequate human reason is to cope with such an intricate human situation. Since the best intentions cannot avert the impending catastrophes, rationality is useless. Thus, the insanity of Fan-i and Shih-p'ing is as much a result of an annulment of human intelligence as of the tragic events. Where rationality ends, mystery begins. Hence, the church music in the background, the living room converted into a church, the nuns who serve as nurses.

Thus, the Prologue and the Epilogue are essentially extensions of the major incidents. Since the main plot is complete in itself the need for an extension seems questionable. Although the playwright himself has argued for the inclusion of the extra parts, directors have tended to ignore them in order to curtail playing time and the size of casts. With or without these parts, however, *Thunderstorm* is a powerful tragedy showing the over-whelming and punitive power of an unknowable natural force, urging men to abide by the principles of justice, and, by implication, denouncing the traditional Chinese family system which tends to complicate unduly human relationships.

CHAPTER 3

Sunrise

DESPITE Fang Ta-sheng's advice, Ch'en Pai-lu, an attractive prostitute, refuses to give up her life of decadence and get married. Sardonic yet kindhearted, she offers food and protection to The Shrimp, a girl about fifteen years old, who has escaped into her hotel suite to avoid being molested by Chin Pa, a powerful plutocrat. The Shrimp, however, is soon kidnapped and sold to a dingy bawdy-house where she finally ends her misery by hanging herself.

Pan Yueh-t'ing, banker and patron of Ch'en Pai-lu, is practically blackmailed into giving his crafty subordinate, Li Shih-ch'ing, a big promotion. When his speculation in government bonds promises a sizable profit, Pan dismisses Li and thus shatters his family life. Huang San, another dismissed employee, seeks in vain to regain his job. He finally commits suicide after having poisoned his children. The price of the bonds, completely manipulated by Chin Pa, soon plummets. Pan subsequently becomes bankrupt. Weary of her life, Ch'en Pai-lu commits suicide by taking sleeping pills. Fang Ta-sheng, unaware of her death, leaves her in order to dedicate himself to fighting against Chin Pa and the powerful and for the downtrodden.

Written in 1936, *Sunrise* is a social problem play which studies evil and suffering in a large Chinese city and suggests the need to rebel against the ruling plutocrats. Because of the censorship and other pressures which *Thunderstorm* had encountered, Ts'ao Yü intimates in his postscript to *Sunrise* that he has minced words in his second play.[1] He says that he has been tempted to imitate Shaw and write a long essay like *The Revolutionist's Handbook*, but personal taste and what he describes as lack of talent have made him content to use a series of eight quotations as a kind of preface.[2] These quotations and the order in which they appear, he says, are significant to an understanding of what he wishes to convey in the play proper but cannot.[3] Since the play-

44

wright has attached so much significance to these quotations, it is useful to examine them briefly before proceeding to the play itself.

The first quotation is from Lao Tzu:

> For thus the way of God
> Cuts people down when they have had too much
> And fills the bowls of those who are in want.
> But the way of man will not work like this:
> The people who have not enough are despoiled
> For tribute to the rich and surfeited.[4]

The other quotations are taken from the Old and New Testaments and include passages which assert that death is the reward of sin and immoral deeds, that people should earn their living by hard work, and that god-fearing men should unite and never abandon hope and faith. The last quotation is taken from the Book of Revelations: "And I saw a new heaven and a new earth. For the first heaven and the first earth passed away, and the sea is no more."[5] Despite the episodic and incoherent organization of these quotations, they are clearly indicative of Ts'ao Yü's vehement attitude about "the way of man" or "the first heaven and the first earth" in which the poor are exploited by the rich and injustice runs rampant, while asserting his faith in the ultimate emergence of a new heaven and a new earth, in which justice and "the way of God" will prevail.

The ideas embodied in the play parallel closely those conveyed in the quotations, although attention is focused on man's way, which permits the rich and surfeited to despoil the needy. The characters and events are chosen and organized in such a way as to illustrate that in a society where man's way prevails, no men except those of extreme wealth can be secure. At the end, through a major character's decision to struggle against social injustice, the play hints at a new way of life. *Sunrise* thus has many characteristics of a problem play since it deals with serious social conditions, attempts to frame our opinions about their nature, and suggests possible solutions.

The play opens with the arrival of Fang Ta-sheng, a school teacher from a remote country place, to visit his former lover Ch'en Pai-lu, a high-class prostitute living in a luxuriously furnished hotel suite in a large city. For the affection that he still bears her and, later, out of an altruistic concern for her well-being, Fang urges Ch'en to leave her decadent city life and go with him to the countryside. Reminiscent of Celimène, who rejects her misanthropic lover Alceste's proposal of marriage and retreat to rural seclusion, Ch'en merely sneers at her admirer's idyllic and naive suggestions. Later events will reveal that she has lived in the country for a year or so while married to a poet, but poverty, loneliness, and the death of their child ruined the marriage. From this sad experience of short-lived happiness and a broken marriage, she has realized that rural seclusion as a means of escape from reality is tantamount to self-exile, a way of life hard for most people to sustain. Though marriage is out of the question, Ch'en asks Fang to spend a few days with her before he returns to his country school. As a result, many evils and miseries in metropolitan life are conveniently seen through this intelligent outsider.

The first important complication arises with Ch'en's discovery of The Shrimp,[6] an orphan about fifteen years old, who has escaped into her suite from another, where she has been tortured because she refuses Chin Pa's illicit advances. Ch'en and Fang offer her protection, but soon she is abducted from Ch'en's suite. Fang's search for her leads to the second important complication, which gives him an opportunity to observe the miseries of a dingy bawdy-house, which, combined with his impression of the life in Ch'en's hotel suite, brings a complete reversal in his attitude.

Before delving into these complications, it is necessary to discuss two invisible but thematically important characters. One is the pursuer of The Shrimp, Chin Pa, whose name means Gold the Eighth; the other is Ch'en Pai-lu's divorced husband, the poet. From Ch'en Pai-lu's experience with the poet, Fang learns that retreat into the countryside is merely idyllic escapism. Because of his knowledge of Chin Pa, Fang realizes that it is persons like Gold the Eighth who cause social problems and miseries. Though Chin Pa never appears, his influence is nearly omnipresent. He has such large current deposits in banks that their withdrawal may strain or even drain the banks' reserves; he holds countless shares of stocks and, because of his abundant cash, can virtually control stock market prices; he employs gangsters who, with impunity, carry out his orders to kidnap his enemies. He is, in short, a threat to the economic well-being and security of other citizens. After he has seen the widespread sufferings in the city, the hermit's life no longer appeals to Fang. On the other hand, if he stays in the city, as he eventually decides to do, he must face the threat of Chin Pa.

In this thematic framework, the incidents serve largely as a series of discoveries which lead to a final reversal: Fang decides to stay in the city and fight Chin Pa. On the surface, the arrangement of these incidents may seem episodic, yet it has a special power since it consists of a series of theses and antitheses, or points and counterpoints. Through contrast, each component pair is given a thematic unity; by intertwining these pairs, the play's central idea is forcefully presented. For example, Ch'en Pai-lu's luxurious hotel suite is contrasted with the dingy bawdy-house to which The Shrimp is taken after her abduction. In terms of characterization, the sophisticated Ch'en is the antithesis of the innocent The Shrimp; Gold the Eighth is the antithesis of the poet, Ch'en's former husband. Generally, the rich are contrasted with the poor, and the honest are counterbalanced by the devious. The following discussion will examine these pairs and the ways in which they advance the central idea.

Overshadowed by Chin Pa, but still the wealthiest character who actually appears in the play, is Pan Yüeh-t'ing, manager of a bank and patron of Ch'en Pai-lu. Because of a recent economic depression, Pan has lost a great deal of money. In order to mislead the public and retain its confidence, he undertakes to construct a skyscraper, while, in order to recoup his losses, he speculates in government bonds. When the play begins, his strategies seem to be working and he therefore can afford to pamper the high-class prostitute, Ch'en Pai-lu.

Of Pan Yüeh-t'ing's employees, two of sharply contrasted personalities frequent the hotel suite for different reasons. One is Pan's secretary, Li Shih-ch'ing, ambitious, adventurous, and quite at home with his employer's affluent associates. By revealing that he has discreetly delved into the bank's secrets (namely that its real properties have long been mortgaged and that its reserves for customers' withdrawals are insufficient), he virtually blackmails his boss into giving him a promotion and a raise. As long as the divulging of these secrets would be ruinous, Pan Yüeh-t'ing helplessly pampers his treacherous employee; but as soon as he feels secure, he ruthlessly dismisses what he terms a "self-opinionated" and "uneducated third-rate" assistant.

The other employee is a minor clerk, Huang Hsing-san, who

has worked in the bank diligently and honestly for four or five years but has recently been dismissed for no reason other than the decline of the bank's business. He gets no compensation, nor has he any savings; yet he has a large family to support. Therefore, he repeatedly attempts to see the manager in order to beg him for a job that pays a meager thirteen dollars a month. What he eventually gets is a stunning blow in the chest and three dollars for compensation. He uses two of them to pay his arrears in rent and the remaining one to buy opium, enough to kill his three children, but insufficient to bring about his own death. He goes insane and finally commits suicide by jumping from a high building, as his fellow employee Li Shih-ch'ing has suggested.

Both Huang and Li eventually share the same fate of unemployment and broken homes despite their divergent natures and the different courses they have followed in seeking to avert their fates. Their misfortune thus suggests the conclusion that, in a plutocratic society, no matter whether one is honest or dishonest, self-assertive or self-effacing, sophisticated or naive, no employee can be assured of permanent employment and freedom from want.

The conclusion can be enlarged to include self-employed professional people, such as Pan Yüeh-t'ing, for he finally falls into the trap set by Chin Pa and is bankrupt. His downfall is even more disastrous than his employees', as Li Shih-ch'ing bitterly points out:

As you say, a pauper. But before you say that you'd better have a look at yourself, my dear Mr. Pan. I'm not in debt, I'm not tens of thousands of dollars in debt. I haven't got people pressing me for money. I haven't had money snatched from under my very nose, just as I was thinking it was mine. You'd better start feeling sorry for yourself, Mr. Pan. You don't even qualify as a pauper. I was made a fool of by a scoundrel, and I'm just poor, but you've been made a fool of by an even greater scoundrel, and he's after your blood.[7]

With the failures of these men comes a variety of sufferings for their wives. While Pan Yüeh-t'ing's married life is appropriately shunned in the hotel suite of his mistress, he has had grievous concern for his "large family" while he is deep in financial trouble.[8] Now that he is bankrupt and ready to commit suicide, the sorrow and destitution that his large family will suffer is imaginable without being spelled out. The wife of the minor clerk, after his dismissal, is finally compelled by hunger and despondency to desert her husband and children after years of a wretched married life. Unlike the clerk's wife, Mrs. Li Shih-ch'ing is devoted to her husband and child, yet at the end her husband loses his job and her child dies for lack of proper and prompt medical treatment. Thus Mrs. Li and Mrs. Huang share the same misfortune of dislocated domestic life, though they are as sharply contrasted in character and temperament as their husbands are. No matter whether a man is honest or dishonest or whether a wife is devoted or not, as long as Chin Pa dominates, domestic dislocations, along with unemployment and business debacles, are inevitable.

The misfortune of these married women— Mrs. Li, Mrs. Huang, and Mrs. Pan—is thematically united with the misfortune of three prostitutes—Ch'en Pai-lu, Ts'ui-hsi, and The Shrimp. At one point, Ts'ui-hsi says that the only hope for a street girl is to find a suitable man and marry him. Ts'ui-hsi is entitled to her opinion, but the incidents in the play do not permit such a rosy hope. In the first place, her own marriage does not bear out her overly optimistic prediction. Her husband and children live a life of misery on her meager and disgraceful income. In the second place, even if Ch'en Pai-lu or The Shrimp can find a better man, all she can reasonably expect is to become a Mrs. Li Shih-ch'ing, a Mrs. Huang Hsing-san, or, at most, a Mrs. Pan Yüeh-t'ing, whose lots are far from desirable. Consequently, in a plutocratic society, marriage is not a desirable alternative for street girls and they must either sink or swim as they are.

Within the group of prostitutes, each is a counterpoint to the other. Ch'en Pai-lu is living in the luxurious hotel suite, while Ts'ui-hsi is settled in a dingy bawdy-house named Precious Harmony. These two places are tied together structurally by the complication in which The Shrimp is abducted from the luxurious hotel to the dingy bawdy-house by Chin Pa's men. This complication, however, is not causally related to the resolution, for the action develops smoothly from the exposition to the dénouement without this complication. Consequently, many directors have deleted Act Three, which takes place in the bawdy-house, and narrate this complication.

Thematically, however, Act Three is essential to the central

idea, as well as indispensable for rendering the resolution
believable. In the resolution, Ch'en Pai-lu, after having learned
that her wealthy admirer Pan has gone bankrupt, commits suicide by taking sleeping pills. Though she is pressed by debtors,
one critic has observed, her suicide is not adequately motivated,
for she could easily find another wealthy supporter to pay
her bills. Thus, this critic concludes that Ch'en's death shows
the playwright's conventional morality, which demands severe
punishment for a prostitute.[9] This criticism is unsatisfactory for
two reasons: it makes Ch'en's death unrelated to the central
idea, and it fails to take into consideration the whole of Act
Three.

The major characters in Act Three are The Shrimp and Ts'ui-
hsi, a prostitute about thirty years old. Like Ch'en Pai-lu, Ts'ui-
hsi is kindhearted and deeply moved by the misfortune of the
newcomer. Like Ch'en Pai-lu, Ts'ui-hsi was extremely popular
a few years ago. She recalls: "When I first came into this
business, I was queen of them all and I saw shining silver dollars by the thousand."[10] But her golden age has long passed;
now she is willing, and indeed, glad, to sell her body at a cheap
price for the satisfaction of any man's carnal pleasure. She cannot help lamenting: "God, it gets worse every day. I don't know
how I can stick at this game a minute longer."[11]

What Ts'ui-hsi was is what Ch'en Pai-lu is—popular and earn-
ing abundant money easily; what Ts'ui-hsi is is what Ch'en Pai-lu
will be, decrepit and undesirable. Similarly, if The Shrimp chooses
to follow in their footsteps, she will no doubt become a popular
Ch'en Pai-lu and then degenerate into a decrepit Ts'ui-hsi. These
three women, at the approximate ages of sixteen, twenty-two, and
thirty, represent the budding, blooming, and rapid decline of
a prostitute.

Without the misfortune of Ts'ui-hsi, Ch'en's suicide might
seem ill-advised, for, as that critic has pointed out, though
her wealthy patron is bankrupt, she is likely to find another
one. Yet, in light of Ts'ui-hsi's misfortune, to find another patron is but to prolong her decadent life a few more years, for
eventually Ch'en will become another Ts'ui-hsi. For the same
reason, The Shrimp chooses to hang herself rather than "receive
guests." In an alternate version, The Shrimp is shown wavering
on the verge of hanging herself. Either version will not alter

substantially the meaning of the whole episode, for both constitute a severe condemnation of the plutocratic society.

Act Three, furthermore, provides a horizontal development of the action in that it extends the applicability of the play. The characters in the Precious Harmony, in addition to The Shrimp and Ts'ui-hsi, are mostly news peddlers, beggars, fruit sellers, and prostitutes. Like characters in Gorky's *The Lower Depths*, these are dregs of humanity to whom hunger and cold are dreadful but daily threats. In sharp contrast, visitors to Ch'en's luxurious hotel suite are wealthy and powerful people. They include Mrs. Ku, a middle-aged widow who has inherited a large fortune from her husband and is now doting on a dandified gigolo, Hu Ssu. Another admirer of Ch'en Pai-lu is George Chang, a nest-feathering government official. All of them are sensual, vulgar, frivolous, causing Fang Ta-sheng to protest to Ch'en: "These friends of yours looked mad to me, every one of them."[12] These people's sleek appearance and frivolous pleasure-making, contrasted with the pale faces and acute suffering of the poor people in Act Three, advance the central idea that in a society where man's way dominates, "The people who have not enough are despoiled for tribute to the rich and surfeited."

The presence of the poor people in Act Three indicates widespread poverty and suffering. In Act One, when The Shrimp, in order to get something to eat, decides to return to Chin Pa, Ch'en Pai-lu is moved to ask: "Can hunger force people to such a degree?"[13] When Fang Ta-sheng, in search of the abducted The Shrimp, visits the Precious Harmony and other similar places, he discovers to what a degree a whole segment of society can be reduced by hunger and cold. Whereas Ch'en can easily feed The Shrimp with her own income, nothing short of social action can solve the problem of widespread poverty. Act Three shows the inadequacy of individual charity and suggests the necessity of social reform.

Where this social reform shall start, Fang Ta-sheng does not know. He only realizes that the plutocrats such as Chin Pa are a hindrance to reform and should thus be checked or removed. His newly awakened social consciousness is indicated in his farewell words to Ch'en: "I may have some dealings with Mr. Chin, I may run around looking for The Shrimp, or I may do something for people like the bank-clerk."[14] Thanks to Ch'en

Pai-lu, who provides the opportunity for him to observe the injustice and misery in metropolitan life, Fang Ta-sheng has undergone a complete reversal in his attitude and action. He has renounced the pursuit of a serene kind of personal happiness and fulfillment in a tranquil countryside, electing rather to stay in the city either to fight against the "rich and surfeited" or to help "the people who have not enough." He is, in short, dedicated to the cause of God's way as against the domination of Man's way.

Ch'en Pai-lu, who has lived in the city longer than Fang, must have realized the necessity of social reform. But, she sees no chance of overcoming Chin Pa. As she tells Fang Ta-sheng: "It is not a question of whether we allow Chin Pa to go on living; it's a question of whether he'll allow us to go on living."[15] With such a fatalistic view of social reform on the one hand and with a bleak view about her future under the status quo, Ch'en Pai-lu is foredoomed.

The actual socio-political circumstances under which *Sunrise* was written could not warrant any optimistic predictions concerning social and economic reforms; nor would the dramatic action thus far unfolded be conducive to simplistic solutions. But whereas Ch'en Pai-lu is sure to die, Fang Ta-sheng has yet a chance to succeed, no matter how slight. This significant contrast is embodied in the climax, in which Ch'en Pai-lu, after having taken an overdose of sleeping pills, is dying in her bedroom, while Fang Ta-sheng makes a last plea outside the locked door:

Listen while I tell you something, Chu-chun [Ch'en Pai-lu]. If you go on living like this you'll be digging your own grave. Now listen, why not go with me after all, instead of tying yourself to those people? Now what about it? Look (*pointing out of the window*) the sun's shining, it's spring. (*The singing of the labourers is now coming nearer. They are singing: "The sun comes up from the east; the sky is a great red glow . . ."*)[16]

The contrast of fortune between an optimistic social reformer and a fatalist is reinforced by stage lighting. Whereas Fang stands in a pool of sunshine which grows brighter and brighter, Ch'en is lying in a dark corner where artificial lights are off and sunshine can hardly filter through the thick curtains. In this way, lighting has been symbolically used throughout the play.

Act Two, which presents the bank clerk's protest and The
Shrimp's abduction, takes place in the murky evening. Act
Three, which presents the suicides of The Shrimp and the bank
clerk, takes place in the darkness of night. Though Act One
opens at dawn as Act Four does, in that act Ch'en and Fang
are exhausted and ready to retire and lighting is appropriately
subdued, whereas in Act Four Fang is standing in a sunlit hall,
with ever-brighter sunshine streaming on his face.

Several times in the play, Ch'en Pai-lu quotes or has other
characters read from her poet-husband's novel, *Sunrise*: "The
sun is risen, and the darkness is left behind. But the sun is not
for us, for we shall be asleep." These lines have foreshadowed
her death and, at the end of the play, become an appropriate
dirge for her. The sun, as indicated by stage directions and borne
out by the dramatic action, is for Fang Ta-sheng, who has
enough sympathy for the downtrodden, enough intelligence to
diagnose the social malaise, and ample courage to fight Chin
Pa and men like him.

Thus, through literary and theatrical devices, *Sunrise* has
forcefully presented the germinal idea derived from Lao Tzu.
As Lao Tzu used them, God's way and Man's way are indeed
vague and general ideas insufficient as guidelines for socio-
political reforms, but their inadequacy enhances rather than reduces the play's esthetic achievement. For a social problem
play, it is less important to specify what is to be done than to
stress that something must be done. Some of the most pathetic
situations in *Sunrise* might be relieved by social legislation; for
instance, an unemployment compensation law might assist the
dismissed bank clerk, and stringent stock market regulations
might restrain speculation and manipulation. But Ts'ao Yü
does not suggest such remedies; he contents himself with being
a social critic, pointing out the social evils that he has observed
and even investigated, and with endeavoring to arouse social
conscience through the only medium at the disposal of a playwright.

The structure of *Sunrise* marks a sharp departure from that
of *Thunderstorm* and is never repeated in Ts'ao Yü's later works.
Ts'ao Yü was aware of the techniques employed, though he
seems to regard them as experimental instead of legitimate and
established methods:

I wanted to break the limitations of "La pièce bien faite" and explore
a new approach, even just for once. Therefore, when I wrote *Sunrise*,
I decided to abandon the structure of *Thunderstorm* and not to
concentrate on a few characters. I wanted to use the fragmentary
method for *Sunrise*, in which a certain conception is expounded
through slices of human life. If the play has any what we would
call "structure," that "structure" is pulled together by that basic
conception,—"The people who have not enough are despoiled for
tribute to the rich and surfeited,"—already noted in the first quotation. The so-called "unity of structure" is to be found in this
quotation.[17]

Actually, as many literary scholars have noted, a play may
be unified in one or in all of three ways: incidents, character, or
thought.[18] Brecht's *The Private Life of the Master Race* is a
series of disjunctive scenes held together only because each
scene illustrates the inhumanity of the Nazi ideology. *Sunrise*,
however, recalls the structure of Ostrovski's *The Storm* more
than that of any other play. "Taking complete advantage of the
analytical method," Donald Clive Stuart writes: "Ostrovski
created a group of characters who typify the tyranny, superstition, idealism, sensitiveness, the spirit of the revolt and the
fatalistic passivity which existed in Russian life in that period.
Certain minor personages have little if anything to do with the
evolution of the plot, but are indispensable to the picture of the
society represented."[19] While Stuart observes that "Ostrovski's
technique is the foundation of Russian dramatic art" and therefore had a strong impact on Chekhov,[20] Ts'ao Yü will give up
the structural techniques of *Sunrise* and move towards those
used by Chekhov in his "plays of indirect action," a term pop-
ularized by Chekhov's ardent admirer, David Magarshack.

CHAPTER 4

The Wild

CH'OU HU, in order to avenge himself and his late father and sister, visits the Chiao family right after his escape from prison. To his great disappointment, Yama Chiao, the battalion commander responsible for the ruin of his family, is now dead, survived by his widow, his son Ta-hsing, and an infant grandson. After intense inner conflict and despite Widow Chiao's effort at reconciliation, Ch'ou Hu murders Ta-hsing and traps Widow Chiao into killing her own grandson. As policemen are approaching, he escapes into a dark forest with Ta-hsing's wife, Chin Tzu, to whom he had been engaged before his imprisonment.

In the forest, Ch'ou Hu has many hallucinations, four of which present events most haunting to his memory, while the last one is a scene in the court of Yama where Yama Chiao is acquitted while the Ch'ous are declared guilty. In defiance of this unjust judgment, Ch'ou Hu fires his gun and thus attracts the pursuing police. After having urged Chin Tzu to join his friends in a concerted struggle for a just and happy society, Ch'ou Hu commits suicide.

On the surface, *The Wild* is a revenge play in which Ch'ou Hu escapes from prison and avenges himself on the son and grandson of the man who has done his family great wrong. The revelation of these wrongs, the deliberation, preparation, and execution of the murders for revenge, and the consequent guilty feeling, escape, and eventual suicide comprise a large part of the play and hold other elements in the play together. That *The Wild* is a revenge play is also indicated by the name of the protagonist, which in Chinese means "vengeful tiger." The significance of the play, however, lies more in the ideas and social implications involved in the murder than in the personal feud.

The first important complication in the play arises with Ch'ou Hu's discovery that Yama Chiao, the chief destroyer of the Ch'ou family, is already dead. If Yama Chiao were alive, Ch'ou Hu would not have any compunctions after the killing, for Yama Chiao's cruelty deserves punishment. With Yama Chiao dead, however, whether the revenge should be carried out on his survivors becomes a question. Here we have the first indication that Ts'ao Yü is not interested in telling a story about "an eye for an eye," for he has deliberately set up a complicated dramatic situation.

The situation is further involved because Yama Chiao is survived by his widow, his son, his daughter-in-law, and a grandson still in the cradle, all of whom, except the widow, are innocent of guilt. Furthermore, the son, Ta-hsing, is on good terms with Ch'ou Hu, for he did all he could to save the Ch'ou family when it was maltreated by his father. If Ta-hsing is spared, the descendants of Yama Chiao will most likely propagate and prosper, yet nothing short of the extinction of the Chiao family can satisfy the "vengeful tiger," for his own father has been buried alive, his sister sold to a brothel at the age of fifteen and later forced to commit suicide, and he himself has been put in jail for eight years on false charges. The dramatic question thus revolves around justice: Is it justifiable to kill a guil[l]ess friend, along with his infant son, because his father has committed a series of brutal offenses?

Ch'ou Hu is fully aware of the problem of ju[s]tice, but is unable to resolve it for a long time. He undergoes a fierce inner conflict, part of which is objectified and communi[c]ated to the audience through his debate with Chin Tzu, h[i]s paramour and Ta-hsing's wife. Chin Tzu was once engaged to Ch'ou Hu, but after Yama Chiao destroyed his family, she w[a]s married to her present husband, whose first wife had died. [I]t has been an ill-fated match. Ta-hsing is to her a weakling, a mama's baby; several references in the play indicate that he is also sexually impotent. Thus she turns to Ch'ou Hu on the day of his return and entrusts to him her love, her hope, and even her life. Since her interest is identified with his, she is in an excellent position to serve as his confidante.

Three times she tries to dissuade Ch'ou Hu from committing the intended murders, and thus three times the question of justice is brought to the fore; but the question cannot yet be resolved. The question first arises when she perceives the increasing danger that surrounds Ch'ou Hu:

CHIN TZU: You—you should not have shown up.

CH'OU HU (*painfully*): Yes, I should. Now that I have shown up, I can't sneak away. I have in me a feud of ten years; my miserable father, my wronged sister, my crippled leg. Chin Tzu, can't you see what I am doing? If I sneak away today, I can't die without a grudge.

CHIN TZU: But (*lowering her voice*) Yama Chiao is dead.

CH'OU HU (*bitterly*): But he is survived by his descendants.

CHIN TZU: But his descendants have not hurt you.

CH'OU HU (*looking at Yama Chiao's picture on the wall*): Yama Chiao has.[1]

The reasoning, in its circularity, reaches a deadlock. The issue is brought up for the second time in connection with the future. Ch'ou Hu has told Chin Tzu of a region where, in his words, the ground is paved with gold, every day is a festival, and people treat each other as brothers and sisters. Chin Tzu aspires to go there with Ch'ou Hu, but, realizing that they cannot start until he has avenged himself, she laments: "Why can't we be there until we have killed and sinned?" (p. 133). Her lament only arouses his suspicion. When she pledges her loyalty with her life, he is moved to tears, saying: "I feel my father is with me, so is my sister. She—they will bless you" (p. 133). The issue of justice is thus bypassed once more, but her question about the prerequisites for going to the ideal region will prove significant.

Since Ch'ou Hu has thus far been unable to confront the issue head-on and resolve it, his inner conflict intensifies with the introduction of other factors, which will be discussed later. Chin Tzu, aware of his conflict, once more counsels clemency by appealing to his sense of pity. Ch'ou Hu then reveals that he is awaiting an opportunity to provoke Ta-hsing to fight so that the killing can be done in self-defense. But, as Chin Tzu points out, even if Ch'ou Hu succeeds in arousing his friend to a fight, the result will still be premeditated manslaughter, for the very provocation is part of the plot. In a court of criminal law, Ch'ou Hu might use the fight as an excuse to mitigate his crime, but in the court of human conscience, his guilt may become even more obnoxious. Therefore, his decision to provoke Ta-hsing by revealing his affair with Chin Tzu cannot resolve the issue of justice. It serves only to betray his anxiety to justify his intended murder and thus to dilute the resultant qualm of conscience; its failure to draw the expected reaction from Ta-hsing thus puts Ch'ou Hu on the spot.

Additional complicating factors stem mainly from the interference of Chiao Mu, widow of Yama Chiao. She becomes alert to Ch'ou Hu's intentions as soon as she hears his name and takes steps to avert the catastrophe. She begs Chin Tzu not to tell her husband who her lover is, knowing that Ta-hsing will not be Ch'ou Hu's match in a duel if her son attempts to defend his honor. She suggests that Chin Tzu elope quietly with her lover and offers financial help. Even though Chin Tzu regards her suggestion with suspicion and acrimony, Chiao Mu controls her temper and sounds genuinely conciliatory. In her conversation with Ch'ou Hu, Chiao Mu becomes more desperate as she swings from one extreme to another. She appeals to his self-interest, warning him that his life is in danger if he kills; since Ch'ou Hu is the only survivor of his family, the Ch'ous will be totally swept out of existence with his death. On the other hand, if he should spare her descendants, she is willing to offer him all she has for his satisfaction, including her own life. After her attempt at persuasion fails, she first attempts to kill him with her heavy iron walking stick, then threatens to report him to the police if he stays one more day. The inner and interpersonal conflicts during this scene are fierce, and a breathless suspense ensues when Ch'ou Hu stands unwavering in his determination to avenge himself.

After his talk with Chiao Mu, Ch'ou Hu becomes fully aware of the danger involved in the intended murders, as well as of the profit to be obtained by forgoing them. The issue of justice, likewise, receives another thorough examination from a new viewpoint. Despite the danger and dubious ethics of the murder, Ch'ou nevertheless deliberately carries it out. In a scene somewhat reminiscent of the murder of Duncan, Ch'ou Hu kills his sleeping friend and host with a dagger off stage, while Chin Tzu stands outside the room. Immediately he feels the qualms of a guilty conscience and, when told to wash his hands, says: "The blood stain can never be washed off" (p. 162). His revenge goes beyond that in *Macbeth*, however, for he has asked Chin Tzu to move the baby, the son of Ta-hsing's late wife, into the bed where Ch'ou Hu is supposed to sleep, vaguely anticipating that Chiao Mu will smash it with her iron walking stick in an attempt to kill him in his sleep. Chiao Mu indeed falls into the trap and kills her own grandson. In the wake of these double murders, the police, sent for by Chiao Mu, arrive, and Ch'ou Hu escapes into the forest with Chin Tzu.

The action up to the second murder is presented in a realistic style. With Act Three, which takes place in the forest, it becomes expressionistic, as many figures and events, actually mere hallucinations of Ch'ou's feverish brain, are presented. Because of similarities in style, setting, and hallucinatory episodes, *The Wild* has been compared with *The Emperor Jones*.[2] The ideas embodied in *The Emperor Jones* and *The Wild*, however, are quite different. Whereas O'Neill's play is a psychological study of primal and racial fear, *The Wild* examines justice in a much more complex situation.

The last act is so rich in ideas, symbols, offstage sounds, and other elements that it seems difficult to analyze it without overlooking some significant elements. Perhaps it is sufficient to note that two different levels—the realistic and the symbolic—are clearly discernible in this act of five scenes. The realistic level is concerned with the escape of Ch'ou Hu and Chin Tzu, their search for the train station, and their pursuit by the police. The symbolic level is primarily concerned with Ch'ou Hu's hallucinations, which Chin Tzu does not share, except in seeing him act frenziedly and talk to what is to her a dark void. These two levels are actually so interwoven that the action moves in a meandering manner instead of in a straight and logical line.

On the realistic level, the action ends in Ch'ou Hu's death. This ultimate reversal begins immediately after the murder, prior to which Ch'ou Hu is a pursuer seeking retribution, but after which he becomes the pursued. Chiao Mu, the only major character who has opposed his scheme, has by then lost all she cares for and has followed him into the forest, into which the police also have entered. A blind, aged woman, she really cannot do any direct harm to him physically. Furthermore, superstitious-minded, she is concerned more with the evocation and revival of her grandson than with the liquidation of a blood debt. Nevertheless, she performs the function of a Fury and whets the guilty conscience of Ch'ou Hu whenever it tends to dull.

After smashing her grandson and discovering her fatal error, she enters, according to the stage directions, holding the baby's body covered with a dark cloth, her face like a tragic mask. She neither cries nor screams, suggesting the most tortured soul in

Hell, which, according to Buddhist doctrine, is denied the relief
of groaning. Ch'ou Hu, the murderer, and Chin Tzu, his accom-
plice, are compelled to retreat by this horrifying sight, while
Chiao Mu calls Ch'ou's name and bursts into the following
accusation and promise of revenge:

Hu-tzu, your heart is too hard. Heaven will never forgive you. We
Chiaos have indeed done you wrong, but your scheme of revenge
is too wicked. You've guessed right; see, I killed the baby with my
own hand. I am going to take him to the temple and ask the priest
to revive him. If the old master can't save him, I will follow you,
wherever you go.   (p. 165)

Throughout the first four scenes of the last act, the drum in
the temple vibrates continuously, sometimes loudly, sometimes
softly, but never ceasing. Accompanying the tom-tom is the
intermittent invocation of Chiao Mu calling the soul of her
grandson to return. Occasionally, she becomes visible in the
forest, her hair disheveled, her dark clothing torn, her tragic
mask smeared with tears glistening in the light of the red lantern
carried by The Fool who accompanies her. Ch'ou Hu is stupe-
fied by such sights and sounds. "Listen, the drum," he reminds
Chin Tzu on one occasion, "this deadly drum. It is not the sound
by which the Little Darkbaby is invoked; it is rather the sound
driving me to my death." (p. 197).

Chin Tzu endeavors to divert his attention by asking if he
has forgotten his late father and sister. As soon as he answers
negatively, the woodpecker's quick, sharp pecking strokes become audible, temporarily subduing the drum sound. But since
Ch'ou Hu is reminded of his late father and sister, he tends to
fall into hallucinations in which their past miseries are vividly
represented. In this way, the realistic level and the symbolic
level are closely intertwined. On the realistic level, Chaio Mu's
cries and the drumbeat have the effect of stimulating Ch'ou
Hu's guilty conscience, making him lose his way in the dark
forest and become exhausted, until at last he is surrounded by
the police and commits suicide.

As has been stated before, Chiao Mu, a blind old woman, can
hardly overpower the sturdy Ch'ou Hu and do him direct harm.
Yet, her figure and the drum can disturb and frighten him more
intensely than the pursuing police. This fear is primarily moral,
though mingled with a kind of primordial fear such as the

Emperor Jones was subjected to. The purgation of the moral
fear can be achieved either by eliminating the person who fears
or by proving to him that he is not morally wrong. In the present play, the purgation is achieved in both ways.

On the symbolic level, however, Ch'ou Hu emerges trium-
phant after a painful examination of the wrongs he has committed and the wrongs that have been done to him and to his
family. In the five scenes, he has five different hallucinations.
Their content and sequence are significant in tracing the process through which he regains emotional equilibrium. The first
hallucinatory figure is most probably Ta-hsing, while the second
is definitely Yama Chiao's grandson. Ch'ou Hu is speechless
and guilt-stricken during the first vision; but after having recovered from the second vision, he defends himself by recalling
the circumstances under which the child was killed, declaring
that he was under great mental strain after the killing of Ta-hsing
and was not fully aware of the consequences of his action. In
view of the actual circumstances presented in Act Two, his
defense is largely acceptable, although he cannot be judged to
be free of guilt.

He is not even justified by the wrongs that he has suffered.
Thus two scenes are now presented on the symbolic level to
balance the first two hallucinations. These new visions show:
Ch'ou Hu's father being robbed of the ownership certificate
to his land by Yama Chiao and then being buried alive, while
Ch'ou Hu's sister cries bitterly nearby; and Ch'ou Hu being
tortured by the jail guard until he kills him and escapes. These
two scenes, nevertheless, are insufficient to justify fully the
murders. The reasons and argument embodied in them are
practically the same as those offered in Act Two. In the previous
acts, persecution and revenge are contemplated; now revenge
has been executed and the persecution is recalled. Regardless of
the sequence, Ch'ou Hu's murders thus far embody merely an
"eye for an eye" philosophy, a primitive justice comparable to
that reached at the end of the *Libation Bearers*: one senseless
murder is avenged by another. Just as Orestes is finally acquitted
after a symbolic trial in *Eumenides*, Ch'ou Hu, likewise, finds
his peace after witnessing a mock trial in the court of Yama.

In the last hallucination, Ch'ou Hu's father and sister appear
as defendants in the court of Yama, king of the underworld,
who, in popular superstition, is the incarnation of justice in the

life hereafter. According to this belief, Yama can redress wrongs suffered in the human world, detect sins and crimes hitherto unexposed, and mete out rewards and punishment properly. His, in short, is the final court of judgment. If he is what he is supposed to be, Ch'ou Hu's revenge may be deemed a rash infringement on the prerogative of the god, for he has resorted to personal vengeance before he has exhausted human and divine law. But, alas, and to the great relief of Ch'ou Hu, King Yama proves no better than Yama Chiao; furthermore, he is identified with Yama Chiao, condoning the latter's crime, condemning Ch'ou Hu's innocent father and sister, and bursting into sinister laughter with the rest of his court during the travesty of a trial.

Ch'ou Hu realizes, after the last hallucination, that he, his family, and people like them will be denied justice forever, both in this world and in the world of the hereafter. He, and people like him, must take justice into their own hands, striking back relentlessly if necessary. He calls King Yama, Yama Chiao, and their followers swindlers and robbers, spits and shoots at them, as the cock crows afar, greeting the dawn of a new morning. Chin Tzu clarifies the symbol of the crowing, which may be missed by the audience: "It is almost dawn already" (p. 219). Ch'ou Hu joins her in an echo: "Yes, indeed," for in his own mind he has now passed the darkest hours of his life and overcome the qualms of a guilty conscience.

Ch'ou Hu's victory on the symbolic level and his destruction on the realistic level correspond closely to the spiritual ascendance at the very moment of physical destruction—the typical pattern of great Western tragedies. In the final analysis, however, he seems to be free of *hamartia*, either in the sense of an error in judgment or in the sense of a flaw in character. Perhaps he should not have been so hesitant in carrying out the murder of Ta-hsing; perhaps he should not have been so guilt-stricken after the killing; but he would then have failed to gain our understanding, not to mention our sympathy.

In the creation of Ch'ou Hu, Ts'ao Yü apparently has Prometheus in mind as the prototype. He does not use a preface or postscript to explain his design as in *Thunderstorm* and *Sunrise*, but in addition to his characterization of Ch'ou Hu, there is ample evidence in stage directions, costumes, and scene designs to suggest his intention. In the prelude prior to the opening scene,

Ts'ao Yü calls for a setting with a magnificent tree at stage center "erecting in the blue atmosphere of the wilderness, symbolizing severity, treachery, rebellion, and depression, like Prometheus bound to the cliff" (p. 9). Ch'ou Hu is standing before this tree, when the curtain rises, his feet bound by fetters. The last scene takes place in the same spot, and Ts'ao Yü once more describes the magnificent tree as severe in appearance, "like a rebellious soul" (p. 221). The fetters which Ch'ou Hu once wore and broke are still there, moving him to observe that "these things which I broke the other day will be put on me again" (p. 228). Ch'ou Hu, of course, refuses to be captured and fettered again. In a manner reminiscent of Othello's suicide, Ch'ou Hu says: "Remember, Chin Tzu, after the child is born, tell him that his father is not captured by the running dogs. Tell my brethren that Ch'ou Hu refuses to wear these fetters, but prefers to die, thus" (p. 229). With his last breath, he stabs himself and casts away the fetters, immensely gratified with his attainment of peace and freedom, though the price he pays is his very life.

As is obvious from the last quotation, *The Wild* like *Sunrise* and some later plays, ends on an optimistic note. During the ten days that Ch'ou Hu and Chin Tzu stay together, she has become pregnant. When they are surrounded by the police, Ch'ou Hu fires his last two bullets and then stabs himself to distract the police from Chin Tzu so that she can cross the railroad to the station where she can escape to the region of safety and happiness. Though it seems unlikely that a pregnancy can be verified ten days after conception, its possibility adds an optimistic note and increases the exuberance and sense of triumph of the Promethean hero.

Ch'ou Hu's optimism is further enhanced by his reiterated belief in the bright future and eventual freedom of his "brethren." In one instance, when Chin Tzu thinks that, since the police have surrounded them, they must be finished, Ch'ou Hu says: "No, we can't be finished. If I am finished, there are my brethren; if they are finished, there are more brethren. We can't be suppressed generation after generation" (p. 226). Apparently not convinced of his assurance and reluctant to leave him, Chin Tzu asks:

CHIN (*bursting into tears*): Dear Hu, where do you want me to go?
CH'OU HU (*insistently*): I have just told you.
CHIN: Are your friends reliable?
CH'OU HU: They are my brethren, men of all walks. . . . Tell them
that I have no more faith in heaven or earth, but I have faith in
my brethren. If they struggle together, they will survive; but if
they struggle single-handedly, they will perish. Tell them not to
be afraid of adversity or difficulty. Struggle they must, so that our
children someday will arise.   (p. 226)

The mention of brethren has appeared earlier, particularly in
Act Two, when Ch'ou Hu assures Chin Tzu that their escape
will be assisted by his brethren. Yet, since he has just escaped
from eight years of imprisonment, Ch'ou Hu obviously has no
opportunity of contacting them, for otherwise they would have
freed him of his fetters. This is no mere technical error, either,
for the fetters symbolize the suppression and torture imposed on
him by the existing society; the brethren represent a multitude
who will create a new society. Without the former, the accusation against the old society will be weakened; without the
latter, the confidence in the emergence of a new society may
seem hollow. Each symbol is thus essential to the overall impression of the play, but their combination is disconcerting.

To a considerable extent, Ch'ou Hu's statements about "my
brethren" backfire just as his description of the ideal region
does. The former suggests a universal brotherhood of oppressed
people, the latter a Utopia which does not exist. Thus, they
must be products of Ch'ou Hu's imagination rather than of
his experience.

Ch'ou Hu's world vision parallels that of the Communists.
In Ch'ou Hu's judgment, the oppressed have the right to avenge
themselves through violence, but since the oppressors have force
on their side, the oppressed must unite lest they be eliminated
individually. Ch'ou Hu has struck single-handedly but has failed
to realize that he is right to do so until it is too late. Though he
dies, he finally is rid of his fetters and, more importantly, con-
ceives a message for his brethren. This message recalls the
battle cry of *The Communist Manifesto*:

The Communists disdain to conceal their views and aims. They
openly declare that their ends can be attained only by a forcible
overthrow of all existing social conditions. Let the ruling classes

tremble at a Communist revolution. The proletarians have nothing
to lose but their chains. They have a world to win.

Workingmen of all countries, unite![3]

Communist critics, however, disparage *The Wild*, as is evident
from a summary criticism included in a recently published literary history:

After *Sunrise*, the author wrote *The Wild*, turning his attention from
city to countryside and telling the story of a peasant's revenge against
a vicious landlord, a good subject. But the author did not understand
the primary class contradictions and conflicts in the countryside, nor
was he familiar with the life of the peasants. These, in addition to
his fatalism, made a realistically significant story extremely mys-
terious, extremely abstract, and hardly comprehensible. Occult sym-
bolism, intertwined with inner conflicts and qualms of conscience,
is used excessively in presenting primal fear and a ghostly atmosphere.
As a result, the story is so removed from reality that it is almost
not a story of human beings. *The Wild*, among the author's works,
is a failure.[4]

Perhaps Ts'ao Yü had neglected to read Chapter III of the
Communist Manifesto on Socialist and Communist literature.
But, if he faltered in proletarian ideology, he gained esthetically
—at least by non-Communist criteria.

CHAPTER 5

Just Thinking

SINCE his juggling troupe has gone from bad to worse, Old Shriveled Melon decides to switch to the regular theater, which is thriving more than ever before. Therefore, he writes a play featuring himself, his wife, and his son, in hopes that a successful debut will bring them fame and wealth. The presentation, however, is such a fiasco that all his dreams are shattered. To comfort his disillusioned wife, Old Shriveled Melon assures her that he has better plays to produce. Asked where they are, he says: "I am just thinking."

Just Thinking was based on *The Red Velvet Goat* of Josephina Niggli, a native of Mexico, who wrote her first play while taking a course in playwriting at the University of North Carolina in 1935.[1] During this and the following year she finished a total of five plays, all of which were produced by The Carolina Playmakers and then published in 1938 under the title *Mexican Folk Plays*. The introduction by Frederick H. Koch bears the date March 5, 1938, while *Just Thinking* was first published in October, 1940. Ts'ao Yü proved once more that he kept abreast of new publications and made use of them.

The Red Velvet Goat is about Esteban, who presents a play of his own composition in order to make enough money to buy a goat, only to have his wife, Mariana, spend the meager box-office income on a new red velvet gown. Hence, the title of the play. Previously Esteban has said to his wife:

We only need ten pesos for a goat. Don Pepe said he'd sell us one of his. With the money from its milk and cheese we'll have enough to buy another one, and soon we'll have a flock. Then we'll be the richest two in town.[2]

After his castle in the air has been swept away by the feminine fancy for new clothes, "Esteban grasps his head and moans as the curtain closes."[3]

66

As to the play composed and produced by Esteban, it is described in its prologue as "a tragedy of laughter, and a comedy of tears."[4] To be exact, an unfaithful wife is killed by her warrior husband when he returns home from a protracted war. In technique, it is close to the farcical tragedy included in *A Midsummer Night's Dream*. Esteban is comparable to Quince, and his domestic troupe is comparable to Snug, Bottom, and the rest of the rude mechanicals. Thus, *The Red Velvet Goat* as a whole is scarcely longer than an episode in *A Midsummer Night's Dream*.

Farcical comedies such as *The Red Velvet Goat* are widely popular in Mexico under the name of "sainete." Niggli has not only written in the form of folk drama familiar to her since childhood; she has also based the characters, with the exception of Mariana, on real persons.[5] In her play, she recalls these native folk with fond nostalgia. Consequently, according to Rodolfo Usigli, director of the Theater of the National University of Mexico, and one of Mexico's leading dramatists, "There is a tender touch of smiling maternity in her treatment which gives a peculiar grace to the characters."[6] Of her play, Niggli writes: "If there is a moral to be found in this play, I think it is this: that we may thank God that there are still grown people who retain the hearts of children."[7]

Just Thinking follows its original source quite closely by presenting Old Shriveled Melon, an aging juggler who has conceived the happy idea of making money and winning fame by working in large "spoken-drama" theaters. Like an Aristophanic comedy, *Just Thinking* develops this happy idea by showing how Old Shriveled Melon has contrived to compose a play, how he rehearses it with his wife and son, and how the play is finally produced. To the opening of his play, Old Shriveled Melon has invited a manager of a large theater from whom the old juggler expects a contract offering him, his wife, and son important positions and lucrative pay in the theater.

Not having any experience in the legitimate theater, everything the jugglers do is ludicrous. For example, just before curtain time, they discover that they do not have a prompter and hurriedly seek out Laughter to fill the position. After the audience has arrived and the play is about to start, Laughter uses the occasion to announce the program and location of his entertainment booth and to invite the audience to visit it. During the performance he either reads the lines just one line ahead of the characters or simultaneously with them, creating the comic effect of a duet. The manager of the regular theater, of course, cannot tolerate this bizarre performance and leaves in the middle of it, with the message that Old Shriveled Melon is a fool. Though this result is disastrous to the jugglers, for a reader it results in the most lighthearted of Ts'ao Yü's works.

Among the alterations made in Niggli's play, perhaps the most significant is indicated by the change of the title to *Just Thinking*. Like Esteban, Old Shriveled Melon builds his dreams of a brilliant future on the production of his play. Confident of his literary talent and attracted by the thriving business in the spoken-drama theaters, he envisions the glorious life that will follow in the wake of his big hit. Whereas Esteban can start his fortune with ten pesos for a goat, nothing short of genuine talent can give Old Shriveled Melon sustained success; whereas Esteban can be "ruined" by his wife who squanders the ten pesos on her wardrobe, Old Shriveled Melon has himself to blame for his failure. Thus, while the ending of *The Red Velvet Goat* sees Esteban justifiably furious with Mariana, the ending of *Just Thinking* finds Old Shriveled Melon claiming that he is indeed talented and has many better plays to produce. Asked by Little Sweet Melon where these good plays are, he stammers: "I, I am just thinking,"[8] and the curtain falls as he smiles apologetically and helplessly at his beloved.

In his baffled apology to his wife, is Old Shriveled Melon conveying a message of his creator? If not, why has Ts'ao Yü departed so significantly from the original source after having followed its incidents in detail up to this point?

It is mere speculation to identify the opinion of a character with that of its author. Thus, prudence suggests that it is unwise to assert that Ts'ao Yü, in the words of Old Shriveled Melon, is laughing at himself and promising to produce better works in the future. But one thing is certain: thanks to the congenial influence of a feminine playwright from a semi-tropical land, Ts'ao Yü has produced his most lighthearted play. The vehemence, indignation, and relentlessness embodied in his earlier plays—*Thunderstorm, Sunrise*, and *The Wild*—are poles removed from the emotions embodied in the present play. For the first time, the angry young man Ts'ao Yü has revealed in his work that he can be indulgent of trivialities and can laugh and sing amid poverty and setbacks.

Niggli might have exerted no more than a catalytic influence on Ts'ao Yü's attitude and outlook; in fact, her influence may well have been infinitesimal. His acknowledgment of indebtedness to her is confined to a succinct statement: "The present play is based on the outline of Niggli's *The Red Velvet Goat*."[9] But *Just Thinking* is extremely important in revealing a new attitude and outlook on Ts'ao Yü's part, although his critics have thus far failed to note it.[10] In his subsequent plays written during wartime, *Metamorphosis, Peking Man*, and *The Family*, and in *The Bridge*, published in 1947, Ts'ao Yü was to return to subjects of great consequence. With the exception of *Metamorphosis*, these later works deal with Ts'ao Yü's favorite subjects—the decrepitude of the traditional Chinese family system, and the bankruptcy of Chinese industry and economy as manipulated by speculators. But his views expressed in these works are more subtly presented than in the early plays. *Just Thinking* foreshadows his approaching mature and balanced vision of life.

Just Thinking also raises forcibly the question of literary indebtedness. Critics have often belabored the point of Ts'ao Yü's debt to Western playwrights, ranging from the ancient Greek masters to Shakespeare, from Ibsen and Chekhov to O'Neill, and from Dumas *fils*, Galsworthy, and Gorky to Tolstoy.[11] This view has prevailed for more than two decades, though Ts'ao Yü has denied conscious imitation from the very beginning. In the preface to *Thunderstorm* he has written:

I have great admiration for those people who spent time and energy and an inexhaustible barrage of words to footnote my play. After its recent production in our country, there is an ever increasing tendency to assert that I am a disciple of Ibsen, or to speculate that certain parts in the play are inspired by Euripides' *Hippolytus* or Racine's *Phèdre*. Seriously speaking, I was surprised. I am myself, an inconsequential person. I cannot peep into the profundity of these great masters, just as a nocturnal reptile cannot image the brightness of daytime.

In the past ten-odd years, I have indeed read a few plays and participated in a few productions, but to the utmost of my recollection, I cannot recall having deliberately imitated anyone in any part of my composition. Perhaps I have deceived myself at the bottom of my subconsciousness, like an ingrate slave who has drawn the golden thread from the master's household piece by piece, woven them into an ugly dress of my own, and denied that these faded golden threads (because they are in my possession) used to be my master's.

Actually, to steal a story or a few episodes from others is not mendicant. There are many prominent precedents in which the same story has been treated by great masters, ancient and modern, in poetry, drama, novels, and romance. However, if I am to keep a poker face and coldly (though a writer's prejudice always disables him for the task) analyze my own work, I will repeat that when I wrote *Thunderstorm*, I did not imitate any work or works, though I realize that to be able to emulate great masters in power and beauty, even to an inconsiderable degree, would be my greatest glory.[12]

Strange as it may seem, critics have repeatedly quoted portions of this statement out of context to prove that Ts'ao Yü has stolen techniques from Western masters but has denied his indebtedness.[13] The only dramatist for whom Ts'ao Yü has expressed great admiration is Chekhov. The pertinent passages, included in the Postscript to *Sunrise*, are these:

After I finished writing *Thunderstorm*, I gradually became weary of it. I am disgusted with its structure, which seems too "theatrical." Technically, I have overdone. I have the nauseating feeling whenever I read *Thunderstorm* again, that I am satiated with the crude "tricks" which I was so anxious to manipulate. I want to write something in a straightforward manner, to smash the superficial techniques I once picked up, and to conscientiously learn something of greater depth.

I remember a few years ago how I was fascinated and intoxicated by the profundity of Chekhov's art, and how my heavy heart was moved by his plays! After reading *Three Sisters*, I shut my eyes; before me was spreading out a scene of autumnal melancholy, in which Masha, Irina, and Olga, the three sisters with large eyes, sadly leaned together and listened with moist sorrow floating in their eyes, to the cheerful march played from a distance outside the window. The music, charged with the delight of a buoyant life, became fainter and fainter as it went slowly away, and finally faded into emptiness and stillness, as if the eldest sister Olga were murmuring at the doldrums of the life and the uncertainty of hope, their fruitless work, and their meaningless existence. Then emerging tears gradually blurred my eyes, and I was no longer able to lift up my head.

But this great play shows no exaggeration or extravagance of its characters; they are alive, they are living people with palpable souls. Having no exciting scenes, its structure is quite plain, and its plot and characters have little change or development. Nevertheless, it so firmly grasped my soul that I was almost suffocated and caught in a trance of that plaintive atmosphere.[14]

Following this passage is an admission that he has attempted to write in the Chekhovian manner and, dissatisfied with the results, has burned what he had composed. Even if he had succeeded in his emulation to a considerable degree, he said, "whether our present audience would like to see them is still a problem. They want stories, interweavings, and intense scenes; all of these things were missing in the pieces I have burned."[15]

The lengthy quotations from the preface to *Thunderstorm* and the postscript to *Sunrise* practically exhaust Ts'ao Yü's own statements concerning literary influences and debts, subjects which have long been emphasized by critics of his plays, and which to a regrettable extent have prevented Western readers interested in modern Chinese drama from examining his plays as original creations. To sum up his stand on the question, Ts'ao Yü has denied imitation or emulation of any Western writer,[16] at least consciously, with the exception of Chekhov.

In his statement about his failure to imitate Chekhov satisfactorily, Ts'ao Yü betrays too great a concern with techniques and an insufficient concern with ideas and a vision of human destiny. The ideas embodied in *Sunrise* and *The Wild* simply cannot be incorporated into the structure of a Chekhovian play, especially that of the mature plays such as *Three Sisters*. To produce any work structurally similar to a mature Chekhovian play, Ts'ao Yü would first have had to acquire a Chekhovian vision of life. Ideas precede craftsmanship.

As will be seen in the following chapters, Ts'ao Yü finally came very close to Chekhov in both dramatic craft and views of life in *Peking Man* and *The Family*. Whether this change is due to the beneficial influence of Chekhov, Niggli, or other Western writers, or whether it is due to the unprecedented national war or other causes, no one can say. What is certain and, indeed, what is important is Ts'ao Yü's dramatic art and the views of life embodied in his later works. What needs to be said at this juncture is that, as the earliest play that reveals a new

outlook on life and a hitherto unknown sanguine side of the
author's personality, *Just Thinking* is an extremely important
work in Ts'ao Yü's career, trivial as the play and obscure as
its source may be.

CHAPTER 6

Metamorphosis

THE wartime hospital where Dr. Ting works is so corrupt and inefficient that this female physician has no other choice but to resign. Before she leaves, however, Inspector Liang Kung-yang, who has been investigating the hospital *incognito*, reveals himself and dismisses the former administrators. Dr. Ting thus reverses her decision and remains in the hospital to serve the wounded soldiers devotedly.

Because of an inadequate supply of medicine and equipment, malaria runs rampant in the reorganized hospital. Upon his return, Inspector Liang attributes the dire situation to the lack of imagination and initiative on the part of the new administrator. To set an example for the new Chinese officials, Inspector Liang exercises his influence and obtains all materials necessary to curb the disease.

Dr. Ting's only son, Ting Ch'ang, is seriously wounded and requires an operation. With great difficulty, Dr. Ting overcomes the psychological hindrance that arises from her intense maternal love and conducts the operation successfully. In a farewell speech to the soldiers, she promises to let her son return to the frontier so that he can join them in a war in which China's freedom and independence are at stake.

Written in 1940, when China's tenacious resistance against Japanese invasion had entered its third year, *Metamorphosis* is an extremely powerful play about patriotism. It resembles Ts'ao Yü's earlier social problem plays in that it deals with a corrupt hospital administration and traces the downfall of irresponsible officials. Unlike the earlier social problem plays, however, *Metamorphosis* revolves around two admirable and selfless characters whose struggle and success form the main-stream of the action. Consequently, exuberant patriotism and practically unbounded optimism permeate most of the scenes and culminate in Dr. Ting's final declaration: "China, China, you shall be strong!"[1]

In the postscript to the play, Ts'ao Yü writes: "In the great
change initiated by the war, we have witnessed the decline and
downfall of the wavering and corrupted people. We have also
seen the pleasing emergence, growth, and predominance of a
new life and new force after incessant struggles. This chapter
of history, written in blood and sweat and profuse in heroic
and pathetic events, manifests the hardship that our national
warriors have encountered on every frontier of their strife, as
well as the desperate mourning of the degenerate class in the
process of its elimination" (p. 299). Such a drastic change
constitutes, to Ts'ao Yü, a metamorphosis comparable to the
metamorphosis of certain insects as they grow into maturity.
Though these changes are painful, the pains should be regarded
as birth pangs instead of death convulsions, since the body
politic will be renewed and reinvigorated through the process.
Ts'ao Yü thus argues that we should be joyful, even jubilant, in
witnessing this change—the dying away of the old and degenerate, and the birth of the new and vital.

Metamorphosis consists of four acts: the first act shows the
inefficiency of a public hospital under the corrupt administration of Ch'in Chung-hsüan and his nephew Ma Teng-k'o; in
the second act, a government inspector, Liang Kung-yang, after
an investigation, decides to make drastic reforms; in Act Three,
the reorganized hospital demonstrates a remarkable progress
in efficiency and morale, but, because the new administrators
lack initiative and creativity, many urgent problems are not
solved until the second visit of Inspector Liang; finally, in the
last act, the hospital reaches an ideal state and the wounded
soldiers who have been treated there are sufficiently recovered
to return to the front once more.

As this outline indicates, the hospital arrives at its ideal
condition after passing through two stages. In the first stage,
the change is organizational—corrupt officials are removed, and
honest and capable officials are installed. For a while, as is
shown in Act Three, Scene One, the new officials work ardently,
in sharp contrast with their predecessors. They prove, however,
to be incapable of coping with an epidemic of malaria because
the hospital does not have mosquito netting to shield its patients, quinine to treat those who have already contracted the
fever, or trucks to transport the uncontaminated to other regions

for preventive protection. Inspector Liang is very angry when he returns and finds this situation. He accuses the acting director of knowing nothing but administrative routine; he then, through a strenuous campaign, obtains within twenty-four hours a sufficient amount of netting, quinine, and trucks to solve all three problems. In this episode, Liang not only solves the difficulties, he teaches the administrator how to mobilize forces that may seem nonexistent. It is only after this attitudinal change that the hospital is fully geared to function effectively despite the dangers and shortages created by the war.

In view of the two-stage reformation, the play is in substance a rhetorical argument divided into three parts. The first part, which embraces Act One and part of Act Two, demonstrates the need for organizational changes and for a new administrative system. The second part, which continues into Act Three, demonstrates the necessity of a vigorous and imaginative mentality, without which even a well-organized and properly staffed institution cannot function effectively. The last part concludes the argument by demonstrating the great contributions that an institution can make after it has been completely reformed. As far as this general scheme of argument is concerned, the play is well constructed and completely logical.

The play, however, has failed to demonstrate how the necessary reforms can be effected. In the first place, the space devoted to the actual means of reform is slight, suggesting that the playwright is reluctant to deal with the question. In the second place, those parts showing the transition from the old order to the new arouse more questions than they settle, thus making the argument inconclusive and even unconvincing. An examination of the way the reforms are handled should clarify this.

It is made clear in the play that Inspector Liang has been given full authority by the central government to take any measure that he deems necessary in order to reorganize the hospital. A character sketch included in the stage directions describes Liang as a fifty-seven-year-old man with unfathomable "wisdom, experience, understanding, and working energy" (p. 120). Thus, in the imaginary world of the play, Liang is tantamount to a philosopher-king, with boundless intellectual and political power, eminently suited to reforming the hospital. The swiftness with which he gets work done, however, is dis-

concerting, for during three days of investigation *incognito,* he
has noticed an unbelievably large number of things and collected
sufficient irrefutable evidence to dismiss the hospital director
and to arrest its business manager. More bizarre, during an
air raid, he directs within two minutes the removal of a large
number of patients from the West quarters, which he knows
cannot sustain the bombardment. Thus, the patients are saved
from being buried alive, and Dr. Ting is moved to say: "Thank
you, old sir. Within two minutes you have done what would
take us four months to do" (p. 150).

If it were merely a matter of establishing believability on
the realistic level, a change of the two minutes to twenty
minutes or so would correct this gross improbability. The problem, however, is more fundamental. On the one hand, the
dramatic situation is supposed to be typical and ordinary in
order to generate the conviction that what is done in the play
can be repeated elsewhere and outside the fictional world. On
the other hand, the dramatic action must be extraordinary and
phenomenal in order to elicit the desired patriotic response.
To overcome these incompatible demands, Ts'ao Yü has resorted
to "magical" metamorphosis.

The same flaw and strained probability are found in the
second stage of reform, in which mosquito nets, quinine, and
twenty trucks are collected within one day and in the midst
of a fierce war. About this episode, a critic has made a devastating comment:

Look, within one night and by the mere directives and letters of
recommendation of Inspector Liang, all three big problems concerning mosquito nets, trucks, and quinine are solved. But is this
possible? A counterattack is being launched on the front; the battle
is at its most intense moment; is it reasonable that the headquarters
can spare twenty trucks for something far less urgent than the war?
Can Chi-nan have so much quinine in store that it awaits their
demand even at night, that it can donate part of the requested
quantity immediately, and promise to deliver the other part the
following morning? Furthermore, is Li-hsien particularly affluent in
material supply and does it anticipate their need in mosquito nets
so that it has a large number manufactured beforehand and donates
them unconditionally upon demand? All these contingencies, if we
care to use our brain and think, are sheer absurd tricks contrived
to cheat the audience.[2]

Despite defects such as this, *Metamorphosis* was an extremely popular play during and after the war. Pa Chin, a famous author whose novel *Family* was adapted by Ts'ao Yü in 1942, recalls how he felt after having read the manuscript of the play at one sitting: "I forgot that the hours were late and that my eyes were sore and that I was exhausted. My heart was filled with happiness; bright light shone before my eyes. The author had indeed brought us hope."[3] In 1948, when the play was produced in Nanking, a critic wrote: "*Metamorphosis*, a serious and true-to-life portrayal of a hospital in the interior, in which the playwright's command of dramatic effects and careful characterization are fully manifest, has evoked consider- able interest in the nation's capital."[4] As attested by these com- ments, the source of *Metamorphosis*'s popularity and critical enthusiasm doubtlessly lies in the play's excellent characteriza- tion, patriotic thought, and eloquent language.

Since the play revolves around the organization of the hospital and since Inspector Liang Kung-yang is the engineer of its reorga- nization, it is most convenient to start with a consideration of him. Prior to Liang's first entrance, information concerning his character and personality is given through the familiar device of talking about him. Dr. Ting forms her opinion syllogistically: all government officials are corrupt; Inspector Liang is a govern- ment official; therefore, he must be corrupt. Ma Teng-k'o, business manager of the hospital, has heard that the Inspector is ex- tremely capable, yet out of touch with the world. At another time, Ma comforts himself: "What Inspector? He is but a man. Treat him with some good meals, offer him a few nice drinks, and then find out his background and origin; what deals shall be beyond our reach?" (p. 55). K'uang Hsi-t'ang, secretary of the hospital, claims to know the Inspector from a more reliable source and declares that the Inspector "has no pastimes what- ever, but is really very solemn in nature" (p. 75).

After this initial preparation, the director of the hospital enters respectfully and announces, "Gentlemen, this is Inspector Liang Kung-yang" (p. 83), but the Inspector refuses to enter, a sign that he is not typical, since he declines to begin his inspection in the principal office. Moments later, Ma Teng-k'o rushes into the office for records and files (the Inspector has even specified the numbers), saying: "This Inspector is really strange. He seems to know everything" (p. 86). The fear of this corrupt official is later contrasted with the admiration of a character whose honesty has been previously established: "I like him very much" (p. 87).

The building up of Liang's image thus far has subtly undergone two phases: speculations that Liang must be either corruptible or too solemn in nature, and refutations of the speculations after certain characters have actually seen and dealt with him. When Liang finally appears on stage, following the servant's formal and perhaps piercing announcement, "The Inspector is here," he immediately dismisses the servant and says to the director with an easy smile: "I am a country man. Every time he announces my entrance, I do not feel my awe-inspiring authority, but rather, I am frightened by his awe-inspiring air" (p. 121). Two of the key phrases in the passage, "country man" (hsiang-hsia jen) and "awe-inspiring authority" (wei-feng) have rich connotations for a Chinese audience. "Hsiang-hsia jen," a man from the countryside or a villager, implies either peasant ignorance or the humble virtues of simple folk, depending on the context. "Wei-feng" literally means an air of authority, a bearing that can inspire awe, or an intangible august quality. Though it often entails affectation and pomposity, it provides a way of assuring obedience. Thus, in admitting that he is a "hsiang-hsia jen" and does not have "wei-feng," Inspector Liang reveals unobtrusively that though he is an official, he is not one of the conventional type. His drab and shabby costume makes him a proletarian type; his easy manners sometimes make people confuse him with his servant.

After the conviction of the corrupt hospital officials and the miraculous removal of the wounded soldiers during the air raid, Liang returns to his paper work. The action proceeds as follows:

NURSE HSIA (*hiding behind Dr. Ting, whispers*): Dr. Ting, this man is the Inspector.

LIANG (*takes out his glasses, about to put them on but overhearing her, smiles benignly*): Don't I look like one?

NURSE HSIA (*shaking her head and smiling like a child*): You don't look like a magistrate.

DR. TING (*from the bottom of her heart, in a low voice*): This is certainly China's new official.   (p. 152)

The subdued yet unmistakably significant pronouncement of
Dr. Ting, herself a selfless and admirable character, highlights
the portrayal of Inspector Liang, the personification of China's
new official: self-effacing, warmhearted, and efficient. In the
second phase of the hospital's reorganization, Ts'ao Yü further
clarifies his conception of China's "new official":

LIANG (*slowly raises his head*): Deputy Director, do you know
the difference between an old-fashioned official and the wartime
official?
WEN (*vaguely but honestly*): I don't.
LIANG: An old-fashioned official, whenever there is a problem
concerning public affairs, knows nothing but writing reports and
sending telegrams. Once the paper work is finished, he thinks he
has done all his duty, no matter whether the problem is solved or not.
WEN: Then, how about the new official?
LIANG: The new official, I tell you (*suddenly bursting into full
energy and raising his big hands*) will raise his two hands, and
under whatever difficult circumstances (*striking the table*) get the
thing done.
WEN (*weakly*): Inspector Liang, will that be an obviously impossible thing to do?
LIANG (*angrily*): What do you mean by impossible?   (p. 209)

Thereupon Liang lists a half dozen possible approaches for
getting mosquito nets, quinine, and trucks. His quick success
is, of course, simply unbelievable in the given circumstances,
but in view of his action on other occasions, Inspector Liang
is perhaps the most amiable and admirable official that Ts'ao Yü
has ever created.

Of the other characters, Dr. Ting is as important as Inspector
Liang. A widow in her late thirties, she has a seventeen-year-old
son who joins the guerrilla war in a faraway region and can
visit her only at great intervals, thus enabling her to devote
herself totally to serving the wounded soldiers. If Inspector
Liang is a philosopher-king in proletarian clothes, Dr. Ting is
a mother-angel in white uniform. The various scenes revolving
around her converge to create the impression of such an image;
or, to put it another way, these scenes are manifestations of
such an image in action. Thus, Act One sees her press Ma
Teng-k'o indignantly for medical supplies; Act Two reveals her
tenderness for her departing son; Act Three reaches its climax
as she transfuses her own blood into a dying officer, even though

she has worked strenuously for a whole day and night; and, finally, Act Four centers on how she saves her own son from death's door through a successful operation.

These scenes are only episodically related, but they progress in an ascending scale of suspense, for at every stage a greater share of her own welfare is at stake. The threats to her well-being, however, are all temporary, and each leads to a feeling of relief and triumph. The situations thus created also provide excellent opportunities to make exultant and emotional speeches. As a rule, the speeches of sympathetic characters, particularly those of Inspector Liang, Dr. Ting, and her son, tend to harp on the theme of wartime patriotism. They maximize the effects of the outcome of the war—permanent slavery or absolute freedom of the Chinese race. Expectation of a good outcome and fear of an adverse outcome are evoked to sustain patriotism as well as to justify the demand for each individual's complete devotion and sacrifice. Praise or disapproval is given according to whether the action can meet this demand and contribute to final victory. Consequently, Ma Teng-k'o is upbraided for his negligence and slovenliness, while Dr. Ting's son is praised for his eagerness to return to his guerrilla unit.

Speeches such as these are abundant and usually quite long, affecting "the representative scale,"[5] to use the term expounded by Elder Olson in treating dialogue in plays, and making Dr. Ting, her son, and Inspector Liang the focus of attention. Consequently, positive actions and patriotic feelings dominate and contrast sharply with the methods used by Ts'ao Yü in his social problem plays. These speeches are justified, however, for they grow out of character and dramatic situation. Dr. Ting's longest speech can serve as an illustration.

Near the end of the play, Dr. Ting speaks to the soldiers who have come to bid her farewell before returning to the front. In previous scenes, whenever she treated soldiers on stage, Dr. Ting has asked them to come to see her before they leave. Thus, there is both an emotional and logical basis for the gathering which provides an occasion for the speech.

Prior to the speech, Dr. Ting has been preoccupied with the operation on her son, whose safety has been of great concern to the soldiers as well as to her. It is thus natural for Dr. Ting to thank them for their sympathy and concern and to report to them that her son is now safe.

The soldiers' cheerful response, which enhances the optimistic atmosphere, is followed by a quiet moment as Dr. Ting tells of her selfish desire to hold back her son:

Five minutes ago, I was thinking that if he was ever to recover, I would not permit him to join you once more on the front, and to accompany you in running risks. For I was reflecting on the hardship that a mother had endured in raising the child, day and night, incessantly. Oh, that a maternal heart should be so pitiably selfish!   (p. 290)

This confession reveals an inner conflict which enriches her character, increases the complexity of her thought, and recalls an earlier scene in Act Two. During the air raid, Dr. Ting has operated on a young soldier, while Inspector Liang has chatted with him in order to divert his attention and reduce the pain:

LIANG (*kindly*): How old are you?
LITTLE SOLDIER: Seventeen.
LIANG: Are you the oldest or the youngest in your family?
LITTLE SOLDIER: The youngest.
LIANG (*recollecting warmly*): My oldest grandson is of the same age.
LITTLE SOLDIER (*feeling attached*): Where is he?
LIANG: Who?
LITTLE SOLDIER: Your grandson.
LIANG: At the front.
LITTLE SOLDIER: Doing what?
LIANG: Fighting the invader.
LITTLE SOLDIER (*smiling and asking in a natural voice*): How can you bear to let him go?
LIANG (*delighted and sympathetic, with a twinkle in his eyes*): How can your grandmother bear to let you go?   (pp. 145-46)

Dr. Ting's momentary desire to keep her son with her attests once more the agony that any parent or grandparent undergoes in parting with children or grandchildren.

Even though the agony is acute and the sacrifice is great, there is no alternative to resistance for people whose homeland has been invaded. As Dr. Ting elaborates at length, the war's outcome will mean either permanent slavery or absolute freedom. With this realization, Dr. Ting overcomes her selfishness, declaring:

Now you are taking your leave once again. Seeing your examples, how can I any longer think only of an infinitesimal self, deny my son the right due him, and refuse to let him go with you? (*stretches out her hand warmly*) Friends, let us live together with mutual affection and love! I hope I am worthy of being a comrade of yours forever. (*Suddenly and solemnly*) Before you, now I swear that I will dedicate my son to our common mother—our motherland! (p. 291)

The little soldier she has treated conscientiously is among the group leaving for the front on that sunny day. Just as his parents have faced the agony of sparing him for his country, just as Inspector Liang has faced the same agony, Dr. Ting finally comes to grips with the reality of the war. Other parents' examples have increased the plausibility of her decision to dedicate her son; her dedication, in turn, creates the impression that parental sacrifice in a war-torn country is universal and necessary.

This speech, like many others, harps on wartime patriotism, the germinal idea of the play. It, and, to a considerable extent, the whole play, eulogizes heroism—dauntless courage, complete devotion, and self-sacrifice. It is thus understandable that many critics have regarded the play as propaganda. For example, C. T. Hsia has written: "The play was much admired because the contemporary audience saw in the transformation of the hospital a parable for China and in Dr. Ting an exemplary patriot who gives everything, including her son, to her country. Yet the play is patent propaganda: Dr. Ting is grossly idealized and the hospital has no correspondence with the realities of wartime China."[6]

Communist critics, likewise, discredit *Metamorphosis* as having dramatized a hospital reform which was impossible under the Nationalist government;[7] the Nationalist critics, on the other hand, read into the play certain pro-Communist sentiments, such as Dr. Ting's son's going to a remote region which vaguely suggests Yenan, the Communist capital during wartime.[8] All these criticisms may be valid, but *Metamorphosis* can be best treated as totally fictitious. As a production of its author's imagination, *Metamorphosis* can be briefly compared with many of Brecht's plays.

Both Inspector Liang and Dr. Ting are certainly ethereal when compared with a legion of earthy Brechtian characters, such as Galileo and Mother Courage, for whom gluttony and

sensuality form an integral part of their lives. Ts'ao Yü has
given his characters admirable traits so that they can become
exemplary; at one point a character is so moved by Dr. Ting's
heroism that he says: "You are really our hero." At another
point, Dr. Ting says to the soldiers: "You are the heroes that
I admire." By contrast, Brecht's attitude is antiheroic, as is
shown by Galileo's lament: "Pity the country that needs heroes."[9]
Ts'ao Yü's exemplary characters can affect other characters
and, indirectly, the audience, and stimulate their devotion and
willingness to undergo sacrifice for the war, which is treated
as a worthy cause. But Brecht is against all war which, in his
judgment, always causes only suffering and devastation. Finally,
in order to arouse the audience's emotion, Ts'ao Yü uses a
number of devices which Brecht has described as "dramatic,"
while Brecht himself prefers "epic" devices so that the audience
can remain partially detached from the dramatic action and
judge it.

Despite these sharp contrasts, a common element unites
Ts'ao Yü, Brecht, and many other socially conscious dramatists:
they all use the dramatic form—the carefully selected incidents,
characters, and other constituent elements—to support what they
regard as a worthy cause. On the surface, Ts'ao Yü's hero wor-
ship and patriotism seem antithetical to Brecht's antiheroism
and pacifism, but both playwrights have used their arts to
advance the cause of humanity. Written on the eve of World
War II, *Mother Courage, Galileo, The Good Woman of Setzuan*,
as Martin Esslin has explained, express Brecht's abhorrence of
war and his desire to influence public opinion to avert the
approaching war.[10] Written three years after the Japanese had
already invaded China, *Metamorphosis* reflects its author's desire
to end the war at the earliest possible date. Dr. Ting's farewell
speech to the soldiers, part of which has been analyzed earlier,
attests to this desire. The rest of her speech, which starts with
her reluctance to part with her son, recalling Mother Courage's
tenacious efforts to keep her children, proceeds as follows:

But at that moment I forgot you. Overwhelmed by the selfishness
of a maternal heart, I forgot our common ideal—a free and independent
new country. (*People looking at one another, in solemn silence; with
strong voice*) Comrades, our present war is a holy war unprecedented
in five thousand years, and our enemies are stronger than any previous
ones. Such a holy war is the first one in Chinese history, and will

perhaps be the last one. If our contemporaries are too shortsighted to see the importance of the struggle for survival, our sons and grandsons will be condemned to permanent slavery. But (*stretches out her chest resolutely*) once seeing and (*pause*) winning, we will have laid down a lasting foundation for a free, peaceful, and idealistic new society!   (pp. 240-41)

When President Wilson mobilized American opinion for participating in World War I, he claimed that that war would end all wars. Similarly, in *Metamorphosis*, Dr. Ting says: "Once seeing and winning, we will have laid down a lasting foundation for a free, peaceful, and idealistic new society!" In this regard, Dr. Ting embodies a universal hope that peace and justice will prevail after war, while Mother Courage personifies the perennial fear and abhorrence of war. Furthermore, since Dr. Ting attaches so much hope to the outcome of the war, she is willing to sacrifice herself, while Mother Courage yields to the human greed that feeds on war. Generally speaking, Brecht's antiwar plays serve the cause of denouncing wars, while *Metamorphosis*, by advocating efficient organization and selfless patriotism, seeks to end quickly a war against aggression.

While *Metamorphosis* is complementary but antithetic to Brecht's works, it is parallel to the mature works of another German playwright, Friedrich Schiller. In *Don Carlos* and *Fiesko*, for example, despite his skill in characterization and his idealism, Schiller often lapses into melodramatic and theatrical effects. Likewise, *Metamorphosis* is saved from being mere propagandistic melodrama by its fine characterization and lofty ideas. Furthermore, as Donald Clive Stuart has observed about Schiller: "His ultimate aim was not a stirring drama. Like many playwrights of the century, he used drama to teach directly certain ideals, such as liberty, and to inveigh against social and political tyranny."[11] Though Ts'ao Yü's characters, such as Dr. Ting in the obligatory scene, seldom speak merely as their writer's mouthpiece, it is obvious that Ts'ao Yü has used drama to disseminate certain ideals and to protest against social and political tyranny. Whereas Schiller's ideas and protests are often set against a background of wars or court strife, Ts'ao Yü never again uses war as the background of a play. The sole exceptions are his Communist-era plays, which were probably involuntary productions. Thus, *Metamorphosis* is a rare revelation of his ideas on war and peace.

CHAPTER 7

Peking Man

O N the mid-autumn festival day, Tseng Wen-ch'ing is leaving home to look for a job. Determined never to return, he invites Su-fang, for whom he bears a profound love, to leave with him, but his altruistic cousin chooses to stay in his family so that she can take care of his aging father and beloved belongings. After much delay caused by numerous domestic harangues, he finally leaves his impoverished family.

Like his father, Tseng T'ing is unhappily married and inhibited by his grandfather's archaic method of education. Through mutual agreement, however, he and his wife, Jui-chen, secretly reach a divorce settlement. The departing Jui-chen then urges Su-fang to go with her, but the latter declares that she is quite content as long as she can sacrifice herself for the happiness of Wen-ch'ing. Thus, when Wen-ch'ing suddenly returns home wing-clipped and when his wife forces him to take Su-fang as a concubine, Su-fang is both disillusioned and humiliated. She consequently leaves the Tsengs.

Meanwhile, in order to save the mortgaged house for her future use, Wen-ch'ing's domineering wife, Ssu-i, instigates the debtors to take Tseng Hao's coffin as a substitute. The old man is reluctant to relinquish the coffin, for he has been lacquering it annually for his own funeral for more than twenty years. Unable to help his family and ashamed of his ignominious return home, Wen-ch'ing swallows an overdose of opium and dies, while his father is mourning over the loss of his coffin.

Written in 1940, *Peking Man* is a study of the disintegration of the already impoverished Tseng family in Peking in the early 1930s. Merely one generation previously, the Tsengs had been powerful and wealthy. But with the downfall of the Manchu Dynasty in 1911, the fortunes of this scholar-official family suffered a traumatic blow. Worse still, the surviving patriarch of the family, Tseng Hao, is too deeply rooted in the past to grasp the present reality. Even though his authority has dwindled remarkably, Tseng Hao still exercises such a strong influence on his son (Wen-ch'ing) and grandson (T'ing), particularly in the areas of marriage and education, that they, too, become maladjusted and victimized.

Divided into three acts, the dramatic action starts with Wen-ch'ing's leaving home to look for a job and ends with his ignominious return and eventual suicide. Since his father is too old and his son is too young to hold any financially rewarding employment, Wen-ch'ing must assume the responsibility of supporting the family. But, unfortunately, even though anxious to prove his manhood, he cannot fulfill this responsibility. Although the kind of employment that he attempts to find is never mentioned in the story, his failure, in view of his character, is almost pre-ordained. But, since his character is largely molded by his father and since his father is still using the same method to mold the thought and behavior patterns of Wen-ch'ing's own son (T'ing), his character can be better discussed later in connection with the family situation.

As far as dramatic structure is concerned, Wen-ch'ing's abortive attempt to find a job precipitates significant complications. Married to the domineering Ssu-i but actually in love with his cousin Su-fang, Wen-ch'ing, on the eve of what he imagines to be his permanent departure from home, admits to Su-fang his concealed love and invites her to go with him. In a note which explains her reasons, Su-fang declines his invitation. Always jealous and suspicious, Ssu-i intercepts the note and makes such a scene that Wen-ch'ing is driven to resume his opium addiction as a means of escape. His father is so furious at discovering his son smoking opium again that he suffers a stroke and becomes unconscious. Previously, in order to maintain his greedy daughter-in-law's marginal deference to him, Tseng Hao has refused to disclose the amount of his bank deposit; but now, while he is paralyzed, Ssu-i looks in his bank book and discovers that his deposit is negligible. From then on, she has no scruples about pursuing her design to grab the remaining family property. She extends her domination over the family's domestic affairs until at the end Su-fang is compelled to leave and Wen-ch'ing is driven to suicide.

Sharply contrasted with events surrounding Wen-ch'ing is

another series related to Tseng T'ing and his wife Jui-chen. Like
his father, T'ing was married at fifteen, by order of his grandfather, to a woman one year his senior. Similarly, T'ing has
fallen in love with Yüan Yüan, who comes into his life when her
father rents a quarter of Tseng's house. Furthermore, like his
father, T'ing is required to read and memorize essays written
in classical Chinese, long since abolished in school. In short,
T'ing is being molded according to the prototype of a Confucian
scholar just as his father, his grandfather, and his illustrious ancestors were. The way in which T'ing is actually treated in the
family provides the missing information about his father's adolescent life; the miserable life and premature death of Wen-
ch'ing foreshadow his son's future.

Age, however, plays a decisive role in determining their different futures. Middle-aged, Wen-ch'ing is thoroughly imbued
with and tied to traditional ideas and obsolete behavioral patterns, but T'ing is still in his formative years and therefore sus-
ceptible to new influences. In other words, T'ing is capable of
change, while his father is not. Through the differing fates of
these characters, the dramatic action demonstrates the necessity and desirability of change, a recurrent theme in Ts'ao Yü's
works.

Although adequate attention is paid to events which generate
and sustain an optimistic impression of T'ing's future, the focus
of attention is on his elders, who are materially destitute and
spiritually bankrupt. Orbiting around these elders are several
minor characters whose comments provide a perspective against
which the Tsengs' daily life can be viewed more clearly. The
first of these minor characters is Nurse Ch'en, the former wet
nurse of Wen-ch'ing. In the opening expository scene, Nurse
Ch'en arrives from the countryside to visit her old masters, but is
insulted at the entrance by a number of creditors demanding
payment of debts from the Tsengs. After she finally gets inside,
Nurse Ch'en vehemently curses the debt collectors. Then, in a
quiet tone, she recalls with nostalgia the affluence which the
Tsengs enjoyed as recently as a generation ago. At that time,
officials below the third rank were not admitted into the Tseng
household, tips from the guests were so handsome that the door-
man could raise a large family and yet buy land and house, and
thousands of silver taels often passed through her hands for
payments that her mistress entrusted her to make. Near the

dénouement, when the surviving patriarch's birthday is barely observed, Nurse Ch'en cannot but reminisce on the way in which Tseng Hao's father's birthdays were celebrated. On these occasions, she says, guests were everywhere in the house, dramatic troupes performed, curtains embroidered with longevity symbols covered the walls, and fragrance from chrysanthemums permeated the air.

Nurse Ch'en's reminiscences furnish a perspective against which the decrepitude of the surviving Tsengs becomes poignant. More significantly, the fame and wealth that the Tsengs once enjoyed prove that their way of life had been worth pursuing. Nurse Ch'en cannot realize the drastic socio-political changes that have taken place since the overthrow of the monarchical system. To a large extent, neither can Tseng Hao. Consequently, he persists in preserving the family traditions, hoping that someday prestige and prosperity will be restored to his family.

As mentioned earlier, the Tsengs have long been educated according to the ideal pattern of a Confucian scholarly official—versed in literature, genteel in behavior, benevolent at heart, and respectful of authority. But the Confucian sage Mencius had said over two thousand years ago that the governors are to be served and that the governed are to serve. All the Chinese monarchical dynasties incorporated the Mencian principle. Thus, prepared by Tseng Hao to become scholarly officials, Wen-ch'ing and T'ing are not taught any practical skills or professional knowledge that can enable them to make a living outside of officialdom. On the other hand, after a lifetime's instruction and practice, Wen-ch'ing has acquired and absorbed most of the merits and defects of a man who can enjoy leisure but who cannot make both ends meet once deprived of a steady income.

Wen-ch'ing's brother-in-law, Chiang Tai, a returned student from the West who has been exposed to the philosophy of pragmatism, makes a penetrating observation which well illustrates the excessive refinement and the impracticality of the Tseng's way of life.

YUAN: Please drink your tea.
CHIANG: Right, to use tea drinking as an example, my brother-in-law is very particular about it. When he drinks tea, he washes his hands, rinses his mouth, burns incense, and sits tranquilly. His tongue can tell not only the tea leaves' temperament, age, birthplace,

and manufacturing process, and whether the water comes from mountain spring, river, well, melted snow, or from a faucet; his tongue can also distinguish whether the fuel used is charcoal, coal, or wood. We drink tea only to quench our thirst, but to him tea drinking can be vulgar or graceful. But what is the use? He cannot plant tea, or open a tea company, or have a tea export business. All he knows is "tea drinking." No matter how refined or artistic, tea drinking is but tea drinking. What is the use? Please tell me, what is the use?[1]

Just as Nurse Ch'en's reminiscences reveal the Tseng's past and just as Chiang Tai's criticism explains why the Tsengs are suffering in the present, another minor character points out what the Tsengs should do in the future. This character is Yüan Jen-kan, an anthropologist deeply interested in the excavated fossils of the so-called "Peking Man." According to him, the vitality and guilelessness of the uncivilized Peking Man offers a ready remedy for the preciosity and fastidiousness that the Tsengs are apparently suffering from. At one point, while a gorilla image is enlarged and projected on the wall, Yüan Jen-kan says:

This is the ancestor of mankind; this is also the hope of mankind. In his time, people could love and hate, cry and shout as they wished. They were not afraid of either death or life. All year round, they lived freely and followed only their own instinct and emotions. There were no bonds of decorum or restraint of culture; they did not know treachery, betrayal, and distress. They ate raw meat and drank fresh blood; they exposed themselves to the sun, the wind, and the rain. There was no such man-eats-man civilization as ours, and they were very happy.   (pp. 114-15)

The carefree life of the Peking Man as described by Yüan contrasts sharply with the dreary life of the Tsengs, residents of Peking, the centuries-old cultural center of China and site of the discovery of the so-called Peking man. Chiang Tai heartily agrees with the anthropologist:

And they were very happy. Right, indeed, Mr. Yüan, your words are absolutely true. They simply cannot be truer. What kind of life do you see us living? All day long, we are either dejected, or complaining. We are always worried about life and death, about making a career, about finding an emotional outlet. Or we are worried about having nothing to eat or no coffin to sleep in. Day in and day out, we keep hoping, but there is no hope.   (p. 115)

Since the Tsengs are very unhappy and worried, Chiang Tai's criticism is a good diagnosis of the causes of the poverty and misery that his in-laws are suffering. Similarly, Yüan Jen-kan's exuberant praise of the primitive Peking Man constitutes a prescription which may lead to reinvigoration and regeneration. Thus, as one critic has observed, *Peking Man* reverberates with cultural primitivism, a concept which Arthur O. Lovejoy has defined as "the discontent of the civilized with civilization, or with some conspicuous and characteristic feature of it. It is the belief of men living in a relatively highly evolved and complex cultural condition that a life far simpler and less sophisticated in some or in all aspects is a more desirable life."[2]

Just as it is obvious that the Tsengs are hampered by their cultural heritage in adjusting to the changed environment, it is apparent that the alternative way of life as suggested by Chiang and Yüan is unacceptable. It is absurd to advocate a return to the savage life once lived by the Peking Man as an answer to the complexity and sophistry of civilization. Similarly, life stripped of all refinement and artistry, such as Chiang's stark pragmatism suggests, would become extremely monotonous and not worth living. A golden mean must lie somewhere between Tseng Hao's traditionalism and Yüan Jen-kan's primitivism, or between Wen-ch'ing's overrefinement and Chiang Tai's excessive pragmatism. Since the dramatic action has integrated all these characters into an artistic whole, the audience is most likely to reach a balanced view towards life through a dialectical process.

Though an adequate understanding of its ideology is indispensable to fully appreciating it, *Peking Man* appeals primarily to the emotions. Through no particular fault except their spiritual stagnation and inertia of will, the elder Tsengs suffer the misery of attrition and death. The fate of Wen-ch'ing is particularly pathetic, for he has not lived a long comfortable life as has his father, nor does he have a bright future to look forward to as does his son. Caught in the midst of socio-political furor, he has little nostalgia and even less hope. As for the present, poetry, painting, and pigeons offer him some idle diversion, but his wife is averse to pets and indifferent to literature and arts. His cousin Su-fang shares his interests and genuinely sympathizes with him, but his domineering wife always suspects illicit love behind their innocent relationship. Life at home becomes to him increasingly unbearable, yet after his short sojourn in the outside world, he says, "Outside, it is too windy" (p. 219).

Before Wen-ch'ing returns home, wings clipped, Su-fang attaches great hope to the prospect of his making a career for himself and living a happy and independent life. She loves him, but her love has been sublimated as devoted and selfless sacrifice. Her good friend and Wen-ch'ing's daughter-in-law, Jui-chen, urges her to leave the house and seek Wen-ch'ing, but Su-fang refuses. First evasive, then stammering, but finally exultantly fluent, Su-fang explains her seemingly unreasonable action:

Su: Will seeing him be happiness?

Jui: But are you happy here then?

Su: I, I can, for his sake . . . (*suddenly embarrassed and stops*)

Jui: Go on, auntie, you promised to have a heart-to-heart talk with me.

Su: I, I will talk. (*Her face gradually beams, a rosy color emerges on her pale face. Her speech gradually gains fluency; and her voice is slightly trembling, because she is deeply moved.*) Since he is gone, I can wait on his father; I can take care of his child; I can keep his favorite calligraphic scrolls and paintings; I can feed the pigeons that he loves. Even the person he does not love, I feel I should sympathize with, and like, and love, for—

Jui: For what?

Su: For even what he does not love was once close to him (*full of joy, she is surprised that the emotion, which she has buried in her heart and has just found an expression for, is so hard to believe.*)

Jui (*draws a deep breath*): That is why you take such punctilious care of T'ing's mother—my mother-in-law—regardless of your own health!

Su: Don't you think she's miserable now that your father-in-law is gone?

Jui: Really, auntie, have you forgotten the way she treated you and is treating you now?

Su: Why remember those unhappy things? If for him, for such a man, for him—

Jui (*can't help interrupting her*): Oh, my dear auntie, why don't you direct your kindness toward something more significant? Why don't you leave him out of your mind? Why do you waste your sentiment on such a useless man, totally superfluous—

Su: You shouldn't speak of your father-in-law like that.

Jui: Doesn't his own father speak of him like this?

Su: Don't, don't say so. Nobody understands him.

JUI: Are you then prepared not to meet him again the rest of your life?

SU (*bows her head slowly.*)

JUI: Answer me, auntie.

SU: Yes.

JUI: Why did you let him go in the first place?

SU: I saw him so depressed and miserable; I felt sorry for him.

JUI: Are you happy then, now that he is gone?

SU: Yes.

JUI: Why do you two live like this?

SU: Don't you feel happy when you see other people are happy?
                                                              (pp. 198-200)

Jui-chen, who has just divorced her incompatible husband by mutual agreement, naturally disapproves of her aunt's self-imposed sacrifice. Therefore, she keeps asking:

JUI: But my good auntie, what is all this for?

SU: For—

JUI: Yes, for what?

SU: For, I don't know how to put it. (*Suddenly her face shows a peculiar smile.*) For, this is the way to live.   (p. 203)

In light of the earlier one, this passage, though short, reveals two basic attitudes towards life. Jui-chen's is rational; Su-fang's, emotional; Jui Chen's is self-centered, while Su-fang's is altruistic; finally, Jui-chen's is based on individualism, while Su-fang's stems from the traditional Chinese belief that man is primarily a member of the family and society and that an individual may be sacrificed for the welfare of others. With her short pronouncement, "For, this is the way to live," Su-fang reveals a fundamental choice and commitment.

No other character in the play exercises a stronger impact than does Su-fang through the reversal of this commitment. It is understandable why Chiang Tai and Yüan Jen-kan criticize traditional Chinese life and culture. Jui-chen and her husband's rebellion against their family, as climaxed in their secret divorce and her decision to abort her expected child, indicates little more than that the younger generation is changing. But rooted in traditional Chinese art and committed to traditional Chinese morality, Su-fang seems one of those least likely to embrace the cause of the rebels. Yet, circumstances compel her to leave the Tseng household as well as to assume a new outlook toward life. Previously, convinced that Wen-ch'ing is happy away from his dungeon-like home, Su-fang has told Jui-chen that she will never leave until the sky has fallen and the dumb can talk. But no sooner have they finished their conversation than Wen-ch'ing returns, causing Jui-chen to remark that the sky has fallen. Shortly afterwards, Ssu-i, pregnant and desirous of securing Su-fang's service, proposes to make Wen-ch'ing and Su-fang man and concubine on the condition that Su-fang shall not claim even this ignominious marital status in public. Devoid of spiritual and selfless love, Ssu-i imagines that the gratification of carnal desires can entice Su-fang to stay. Insulted by Ssu-i and disillusioned by Wen-ch'ing, Su-fang has no other alternative but to leave. If a woman with such devotion, humility, and selflessness is compelled to leave the declined estate, who but the most moribund, slothful, and villainous will stay?

Ideologically, Su-fang's desertion is tantamount to acknowledging the bankruptcy of the traditional Chinese culture. In terms of dramatic development, her departure precipitates the Tsengs' total disintegration. For many years, Tseng Hao has been relying on the faithful service of Su-fang to provide him a marginally comfortable life. But now with Su-fang gone, his life will obviously become more miserable. More importantly, Su-fang's departure completes Wen-ch'ing's downfall. Wench'ing's return home is a betrayal of Su-fang's faith; her subsequent departure registers her disappointment and disillusionment in him. Furthermore, her determination to struggle independently further clarifies his timidity and decadence. Unable to bear the humiliation any longer, he commits suicide by swallowing opium.

Thus, like many of Ts'ao Yü's dramatic works, *Peking Man* has a double ending, in which those who stick to tradition are doomed to suffer and die, while those capable of adjusting to the new reality are committed to seek a better future. Though Tseng T'ing, unlike Su-fang and his wife Jui-chen, remains at home at the end of the play, he has already acquired a new outlook on life. His adolescent infatuation for Yüan Yüan has diminished; his understanding with his divorced wife, with whom he could hardly communicate previously, has been appreciably increased by the very process in which husband and wife have gracefully arranged a divorce in defiance of their elders. A mutual concern, based on an awareness of their plight, prevails in their farewell scene:

JUI (*comfortingly*): We can write to each other frequently in the future.

T'ING: Very good (*tears begin to fall*). (*Outside Yüan Yüan is calling for Jui-chen.*)

JUI (*sorrowfully*): Don't feel bad; many things have to be learned through suffering.

T'ING: Yet how hard it is to reach an understanding.   (p. 191)

Hard as it is, T'ing has reached a quite thorough understanding of his circumstance and can be reasonably expected to make the necessary adjustments. The pity is that when most children of his age, such as Yüan Yüan and Nurse Ch'en's grandson, are playing freely and innocently, Tseng T'ing is learning the hard facts of life and assuming the burdens that even an adult may find too heavy.

In the absence of any specific sin or crime for which the characters are indicted and punished, *Peking Man,* unlike *Thunderstorm, Sunrise,* and *The Wild,* does not seem to indict the traditional Chinese culture and family system. Arranged marriage and the clannish cohabitation of all generations in one household have indeed complicated interpersonal relationships in the family and increased the sufferings of Wen-ch'ing and his son T'ing, but the Tsengs suffer primarily from a failure to adjust. The dramatic action merely points out that the traditional way of life as lived by the Tsengs is outmoded and unworkable, but does not pass any value judgment on that way of life.

In proportion to the relaxation of Ts'ao Yü's attack on the past, his dramatic techniques have gained in subtlety. Set entirely in the spacious living room, to which every member of the family has access, the dramatic action unfolds slowly, paralleling the leisurely life of the owners. The transition from one episode to another is often so seemingly unmotivated that the organization of the whole play may, at first, appear diffused. Actually, because of numerous symbols, the action is so artistically unified that two apparently disjointed passages often comment on each other. For example, Wen-ch'ing's leaving home is consistently associated with things capable of flying, such as pigeons and kites; consequently, the following passage foreshadows his ignominious return home, even though no direct mention is made of it:

SSU-I: Wen-ch'ing, Nurse Ch'en is looking for you outside. Now that you are going away, why don't you talk to her for a minute? Come along, Wen-ch'ing. (*Su-fang looks at Wen-ch'ing, who exits listlessly with Ssu-i. The chilly whistle sound from the flying pigeons. The cracking sound of the passing wheelbarrow. The tinkling of the cymbal of the blind fortune-teller. Remote peddler's voice: "Pungent plum soup." Su-fang stands still and lost. Then suddenly she sits down on a solitary stool and beings to sob. A breeze flaps the painting on the wall.*)

YÜAN YÜAN (*offstage*): Fly, fly, fly yet upwards. (*Nurse Ch'en enters with her grandson whose eyes are still fixed on the goldfish-shaped kite in the sky.*)

GRANDSON: Grandma, the goldfish up in the sky, up in the sky. Oh, gosh, it's dropped to the ground.

NURSE CH'EN: Don't shout. Go out and see.   (pp. 56-57)

Other important symbols in the play include the coffin that Tseng Hao has painted annually with the best lacquer, even though he cannot afford it. On one occasion, he laments that "the future holds nothing for me but a coffin" (p. 128). Yet, through the conniving of his greedy daughter-in-law, the coffin is finally given to a neighbor, the owner of a textile factory, to redeem the mortgaged house. Tseng Hao's preoccupation with the coffin reflects his stagnant and sterile mentality; his eventual relinquishment of it indicates the extent to which his authority has dwindled; and the acquisition of the coffin by the owner of a textile factory signifies the rising eminence of a new class.

One symbol that occupied a prominent position in the original version but has been deleted from recent versions is the mute character called "Peking Man." A truck driver in the employ of the anthropologist Yüan Jen-kan, this "Peking Man" has the features and appearance of the original Peking Man, whose remains were discovered by anthropologists around 1930. Because of his relationship with Yüan, this mute "Peking Man" can believably appear sporadically; dramatically, he serves as a reminder of the strength that the now much too refined residents of Peking have lost. At first mute, he regains his speech just in time to say, "Let us open the door," as Su-fang leaves the Tseng house (p. 223). This points up her earlier declaration that she will never leave until the dumb can talk. One critic, mainly on the basis of this symbol and Yüan Jen-kan's observation concerning the freedom and happiness of the primitive Peking Man, has concluded that *Peking Man* as a whole reflects Ts'ao

Yü's preference for ideological primitivism.[3] With the elimination of the rather crudely designed symbol of "Peking Man," however, the play has lost some of its primitivism and has gained in clarity and subtlety.

In an earlier chapter, it has been pointed out that Ts'ao Yü has great admiration for Chekhov's artistry, but it was argued that until Ts'ao Yü acquires a Chekhovian vision of life, he cannot emulate the Russian dramatist. *Peking Man* is the earliest of Ts'ao Yü's works to reveal his acquisition of a Chekhovian vision of life as well as an attainment of a Chekhovian artistry. The leisurely unfolded action resembling the daily life of the intelligentsia, the seemingly uneventful family affairs which yet lead to dramatic peripeties, the numerous symbols which not only extend the thematic implications but unify the seemingly disjointed episodes—all these structural devices characteristic of Chekhov's mature plays are manifest in *Peking Man*.

More importantly, like *The Cherry Orchard*, *Peking Man* presents the necessity for change along with the inevitable sadness involved in the change. In Chekhov's plays this emotional ambivalence is best symbolized by the cherry trees which are beautiful but which are eventually chopped down to make room for more useful things. Likewise, essentially exquisite but superfluous characters such as Madame Ranevskaya are driven out of their estate by the crude but pragmatic characters represented by Lopakhin. In *Peking Man*, although the prominent symbols such as the "Peking Man," the kite, the tamed bird, and the coffin all tend to underline the decadence and parasitism of the Tsengs, the leading characters, particularly Tseng Wen-ch'ing, are shown to be delicate in nature and refined in taste. Thus, unpraiseworthy as they are, their disintegration cannot but evoke sympathy and sorrow.

CHAPTER 8

Family

THROUGH the arrangement of Feng Lo-shan, a powerful member of the gentry, and by order of his grandfather, Kao Chüeh-hsin is married to Jui-chüeh, though he and his cousin Mei have been in love since childhood. Jui-chüeh turns out to be an ideal wife and bears him a fine son, but Chüeh-hsin cannot help yearning for his cousin. For his happiness, Jui-chüeh endeavors to bring the separated lovers together, but to no avail; and Mei gradually withers away because of sorrow and ill health.

Yielding to Feng Lo-shan's pleas, masters of the Kao family decide to hand over to him one of their maids, Ming-feng, though many of them know that Feng is a notorious sex maniac. Unwilling to be molested and knowing that her lover, Kao Chüeh-hui, would defend her at all cost, Ming-feng drowns herself. Chüeh-hui naturally comes to hate Feng Lo-shan, but in time he realizes that it is a social system that permits a hypocrite like Feng to dominate that needs to be reformed.

Feng Lo-shan tries to arrange a marriage for Chüeh-ming, who subsequently runs away so that his elder brother's misfortune will not be repeated on him. The news of this disobedience and, more seriously, the discovery of his sons' misconduct so infuriates old Master Kao that he has a stroke. He eventually dies as a result of the remedies of quack doctors and superstitious treatment insisted upon by Mistress Ch'en, his concubine.

For the safety of Master Kao's ghost, Mistress Ch'en insinuates that the pregnant Jui-chueh should give birth out of town. Though Chüeh-hui vehemently objects, Chüeh-hsin and Jui-chüeh, for the sake of domestic harmony, bow to the demands of their elders. Consequently, Jui-chüeh dies for lack of medical care.

Family is adapted from Pa Chin's famous novel of the same name, published in 1933 as the first part of the trilogy, *Turbulent*

Stream. Largely autobiographical, the novel indicts the large
hierarchical family system by presenting the sufferings of the
younger generation of such a family under their grandfather
Master Kao and their eventual rebellion against him. The novel
also reflects and records some of the socio-political turmoil of
Chengtu, a large city in the Chinese hinterland, during the
early 1920s. The novel was an immediate success, and its
rebellious young hero, Kao Chüeh-hui, became an instantaneous
idol of students near his age (twenty).[1] Consequently, the novel
had inestimably wide political implications. Ts'ao Yü's adaptation, finished in 1941, was given hundreds of performances with
full-house audiences both in Chungking and Chengtu. While
in Chengtu, according to one contemporary report, "The audience included several persons whose lives and characters were
portrayed in the play. These people were moved to tears as
the play brought back painful memories."[2]

In the stage version, Ts'ao Yü has necessarily eliminated many
of the socio-political events in the original and relegated the
rest to the background. He also has curtailed the novel's concern
with domestic affairs and has concentrated on various aspects
of love, ranging from frustration to fulfillment, from pretended
affection to complete devotion, from maniacal lust to humanitarian charity. Thus, the stage version has less scope but more
concentration than the novel; it has lost much local color, but
has gained in universal appeal by concentrating on a few basic
human emotions.

In the play, if love is decent, sincere, and considerate of
others, it is always treated with sympathy and warmth; otherwise, it is presented disparagingly. Generally, the events involving
the younger generation fall into the first category, while those
concerning the older generation fall into the second. There is
thus a generation gap, with the older generation being criticized
adversely. Because Master Kao and the widow of his first son,
Madam Chou, are reduced to minor roles and are given many
redeeming traits, the differences in generations cannot be used
as a strict demarcation line between good and evil, as is the
case in the novel.

The conflict between the generations, however, is as strong
in the play as in the novel, and the major complications in the
play arise mostly from the older generation's interference in the

affairs of the younger. Since these affairs are mostly related to love and since the love of the younger generation is characteristically sincere, decent, and considerate, the conflict in the action is between truth and falsehood, decency and indecency, altruism and selfishness.

With this general scheme in mind, the extremely complex action of the play becomes less bewildering. The complexity of the action stems from the large family group. Under patriarch Master Kao and in the same compound live the families of his four sons: Ke-ming, Ke-an, Ke-ting, and his eldest son. This eldest son is sick and never appears on stage, but his second wife and three sons (Madame Chou, Chüeh-hsin, Chüeh-min, and Chüeh-hui) play major roles. In addition to these four households, relatives, friends, and servants also appear in the play.

Until his grandsons start to rebel against him, Master Kao holds indisputable authority in the house. For example, in Act Three, Scene One, after he has discovered that Ke-an has been living with a prostitute and has mortgaged the land that this prodigal son expects to inherit, Master Kao orders Ke-an to box his own ears, and Ke-an has to obey in front of his wife, children, and servants. Usually, Master Kao delegates his authority to Ke-ming, his oldest able-bodied son, and Ke-ming, in turn, expects Chüeh-hsin to supervise his younger brothers. As the eldest son of the eldest son in the clan, Chüeh-hsin feels a special duty to the family, and this sense of responsibility conditions to a large extent his behavior.

This line of command and its influence on Chüeh-hsin is manifested in the most important strand of events in the play: Chüeh-hsin's marriage. He has known Mei since childhood, has studied and played with her in their adolescent years, and has developed a profound love for her. But when Mei's widowed mother objects to the marriage proposal and Chüeh-hsin's grandfather orders him to marry Jui-chüeh, Chüeh-hsin is subjected to an intense inner conflict. He cannot forget Mei, yet he does not want to oppose his grandfather, not so much out of fear but out of a sense of duty to the family. Thus, in the exposition, even though the bride is expected to arrive any moment, he is still lingering in the garden where plum blossoms are blooming ("plum" or *mei* is the name of his beloved cousin). His uncle Ke-ming has to seek him out and lecture him, beginning: "You

are the eldest son of the first household. Your younger brothers
and sisters will take you as their example. Besides, your father
is sick. Such a large family not only needs your support in the
future, it needs you to shoulder your responsibility right now!"[3]

Upholding genuine love as the highest value, Chüeh-hui urges
his brother to elope at the last moment, saying that nothing is
too late if one is courageous. But Chüeh-hsin merely says:
"Courage? But I have to think of this family. I cannot be
impetuously courageous" (p. 39). Thus he stays and is married.

Jui-chüeh turns out to be an ideal wife, enabling Chüeh-hsin
to use her as proof that not all arranged marriages are bad. What
sense dictates, however, sensibility may refute. In time, Mei
becomes increasingly desirable to him because she is unobtain-
able. His romantic despair is further increased when he learns
that Mei, after a short-lived and unhappy marriage, is pining
away and has tuberculosis. Thus, self-pity and sympathy for
his first love induce him to break all the bonds his sense of
responsibility imposes on him. When Mei and her mother are
leaving the Kao compound after a stay of about ten days during
which they have taken shelter from a coup d'etat, Chüeh-hsin
importunes her for her address so that he may contact her
in the future. Jui-chüeh discovers her husband's aberrant action,
but instead of being angry or jealous, she sincerely begs Mei
to stay and take over her position. Chüeh-hsin cannot be happy
without Mei, Jui-chüeh says, and she herself cannot be happy
unless her husband is. Though separation from her husband is
painful to her, Jui-chüeh argues, it is better than to have both
husband and wife suffer. Selfless as Jui-chüeh's emotion is, her
suggestion is simply not feasible under the family system. Thus,
its only discernible effect is to move Mei to advise Chüeh-hsin
to forget her and to take more care of himself and his family.
Since Mei soon dies, this advice becomes her last testament
urging him to abide by sense and to forgo sensibility. Though
Chüeh-hsin follows her advice to be reasonable, considerate,
and affectionate in his relations with his wife, his sorrow over
his unfulfilled love deepens.

Even though Jui-chüeh is only Chüeh-hsin's second choice,
during the ensuing domestic strifes of the large family he loses
his second choice as well. This complication stems from Master
Kao's illness and his concubine's affected love for him. During

Master Kao's illness, Jui-chüeh serves him day and night, because she is the only faithful and reliable person in the large family. Exhaustion undermines her health and prompts the premature birth of her second baby. If modern medical services were obtained, the consequences might not be tragic, but by then the old master has died and his surviving concubine expresses a sham concern for his soul. According to the superstitious custom of "blood glow," the blood emitted by a woman in labor will affect the body of her relative and prevent it from entering heaven. To remedy this effect, Mistress Ch'en says, Jui-chüeh should deliver her baby outside the city.

Mistress Ch'en, as a concubine, does not have much authority in the house, but her opinion carries weight because those in a position to decide have no moral conviction or ethical courage. Before Master Kao's death, Chüeh-hui has a fierce argument with his philistine uncle Ke-ming, the highest authority next to the master himself. Instead of being treated by Western doctors in his own clean and spacious room, Master Kao is moved to a dingy closet and treated by monks and quack doctors. When Chüeh-hui asks why this has happened, the argument goes as follows:

KE-MING: You know, this is Mistress Ch'en's opinion.

HUI: Then why don't we have our own opinion? Why should we follow the foolish opinion of an ignoramus? Do you really believe in what she suggested?

KE-MING: Naturally I don't. But this is your grandfather's fate. If we don't follow her suggestion, in case of his death, who can assume the responsibility and the blame for being unfilial?

HUI (indignant): Right, blame and responsibility! My third uncle, who has the real filial piety, the one who is not afraid of blame and does all he can for the elder, or the one who, in order to avoid the blame of being unfilial, let Grandpa be frightened and victimized by superstition?

KE-MING: You are but a child; you are not in a position to lecture me. (p. 226)

The same pseudo-filial piety drives Jui-chüeh out of the city. Chüeh-hsin is too compliant to resist strong opinions, even for his wife's sake; and Jui-chüeh is overanxious to save her husband from making any hard decision. Thus, on a wintry day, she is taken to a damp, leaky farmhouse, far away from modern medical services. Chüeh-hui has by then just escaped

from prison, about which more will be said later, and urges
his brother to be more self-assertive and to take Jui-chüeh to
a modern hospital in town. As has been the case with his
wedding, Chüeh-hsin says that it is too late. Furthermore,
Mistress Ch'en drags him back to the city, for, as she says,
since he is the eldest son of the household, he is the proper
person to officiate at the ground-breaking ceremony for his
grandfather's false grave. As a consequence of all this, Jui-
chüeh dies.

The problem involved in this tangled strand of incidents is
a choice between values. As the eldest son of the first household in a large family, Chüeh-hsin, aside from his own weak
personality, considers outward harmony and unity more important than self-fulfillment. As a matter of fact, his self-
fulfillment, in the traditional view, is to be found in the
prosperity and prestige of the family as a unit. Dissension and
quarrels are obviously not ways to achieve this purpose, and
he ends by sacrificing his own happiness and those he loves.

Chüeh-hsin neither challenges the traditional view nor does
he even question it. It is his youngest brother, Chüeh-hui, who
raises fundamental questions and rebels against the family system
as a whole. With him, significantly and symbolically, the very
Chinese character for "family" is given a new interpretation.
Composed of two parts, a roof with a pig under it, this character indicates a tremendous progress in human culture: from
nomads and hunters, human beings have settled down in a
fixed place with a roof over their heads and the ability to
raise domestic animals. "Family" thus symbolizes an agricultural
civilization, in which those who have lived longer are normally
more experienced and their opinions more reliable. Veneration
for elders is thus as much a recognition of their knowledge as
of their age. But in an industrial civilization, progress is so
rapid that the best solutions to yesterday's problems may become obsolete today. In the transitional period in which *Family*
is set, tradition demands veneration for and obedience to elders,
regardless of their knowledge, but the younger generation,
imbued with Western ideas and modern knowledge, has come
to doubt their elders' wisdom. If the elders were to practice
the moral principles they preach, they might at least win the
respect due their age, but their selfishness, narrow-mindedness,

and licentiousness erode respect. If elders such as Mistress Ch'en dominate, the youngsters, following the principle of bad coin driving good coin from the market, will eventually perish. The Kao household would be reduced, in Hamlet's words, to an unweeded garden where only things of a rank and gross nature can prosper. Chüeh-hui's self-imposed mission is not only to weed his own garden but to overhaul the whole traditional family system. Before he sets out to fulfill his mission, he has already reached the conclusion that "Family" indeed consists of a roof and a pig, but only in the literal sense: a house sheltering a group of swine-like human beings (p. 216).

Chüeh-hui comes to this realization through a series of sufferings, both those of his eldest brother and, more importantly, his own. He loves a maid in the house, Ming-feng, and intends to marry her. Afraid that, if he tells his family, their love affair may be completely suppressed, Ming-feng asks Chüeh-hui not to reveal their relationship too soon. Meanwhile, a powerful member of the gentry, Feng Lo-shan, has secured Master Kao's permission to have Ming-feng as his mother's maid. Though he is president of the local Confucian Society (and a self-claimed Buddhist worshiper), Feng Lo-shan is a notorious sex maniac. In the past, he has taken many young girls as Buddhist disciples and molested them. For fear of being given to this sex maniac and, more strongly, out of devotion to Chüeh-hui, Ming-feng drowns herself. Her motivation is clearly revealed in the following scene:

MING-FENG: I will think of you till my death. Even after my death, I will still be thinking of you.

HUI: No, I want to think of you while alive; I can't think after my death.

MING: To love a man is to pave his way, not to burden him.

HUI: Are these your own words?

MING: No, they are Mistress Jui-chüeh's. Just think, my third master, think of a girl who loves you from the bottom of her heart. She is unwilling to give you the slightest trouble or the least burden. She heartily hopes that you will be happy all your life, and be courageous, struggle, and succeed, as you have just said.

HUI: You have so much to say today.

MING: Did you say that there is a kind of bird which sings all night until it bleeds?

HUI: Yes, that is the kind which gives men happiness.

MING: I wish I could talk to you all night like that.   (p. 133)

At this point, Ming-feng breaks into tears. Like Antigone, though she has chosen a voluntary death, Ming-feng feels that she has not lived long enough and asks Chüeh-hui to kiss her face, which, she says, has been touched only by her mother, the sun, the moon, and the wind. By then the night guard is passing and, with much work to do, Chüeh-hui says good-night to her and returns to his own chamber, touched and puzzled by her emotion, yet unaware of her hidden decision.

Ming-feng's death has a stunning impact on Chüeh-hui and for a long period of time he refuses to speak to anyone, including his brothers, who are very close to him. From his deep reflection he emerges with new ideas, which are revealed when a marriage for Chüeh-min is proposed. Once more, Feng Lo-shan is trying to arrange a marriage for the Kao family and once more Master Kao has consented. If Chüeh-min fails to take prompt and defiant action, the misfortune of Chüeh-hsin and Mei will be repeated by him and his cousin Ch'in. The youngest brother advocates elopement, the eldest brother advises prudence, and they fall into an argument:

CHÜEH-HSIN: I know that since Ming-feng's death, you have completely changed: you hate and you doubt.
CHÜEH-HUI: Just the opposite, I love more ardently, and I believe more deeply. (*Compassionately*) Eldest brother, don't try to explain all of my action by Ming-feng's death. I love her, I really do. After I lost her, I realized how much I had lost; the loss is irrevocable. Immediately after her death, I thought only of her, but gradually I began to see the serious problems raised by her death. (*Solemnly*) I have sworn to dedicate myself to the fulfillment of my ideas and decisions. Perhaps I will be laughed at, and fail, and die. But as long as I live, I will never be bound by prudence.   (p. 194)

The serious problems raised by Ming-feng's death and mentioned by Chüeh-hui include bond slavery, arranged marriages, the patriarchal family system, and the social structure which permits a hypocrite like Feng Lo-shan to prosper. After a new series of sufferings and discoveries, Chüeh-hui will resolve to leave home in order to change these systems. This new series is closely related to Ming-feng's death, for another maid, Wan-erh, is given to Feng Lo-shan as a substitute. Later, on Master Kao's birthday, as a gesture of generosity, Wan-erh is permitted to visit her former masters. After insistent questioning, Wan-erh reveals the brutal behavior of the sex maniac and begs her former masters to take her back; otherwise, she says, she will be tortured to death within half a year. Chüeh-hui is infuriated and later explodes into angry protest when he discovers Feng Lo-shan using a lighted cigarette to torture Wan-erh into confessing what secrets she has revealed. But under the domination of his grandfather, Chüeh-hui cannot even voice his protest, for propriety requires him not to insult an honorable guest.

Chüeh-hui's protest only serves to antagonize an influential man, who has him arrested and sentenced to death on false charges. He is put before the firing squad, but mysteriously he escapes death. This experience enables the young rebel to realize the value of life and the hideousness of the systems which devalue life.

While facing the guns of the firing squad, Chüeh-hui recalls, the first person that came to his mind was his eldest brother, whose compliant attitude had once driven Chüeh-hui to the extreme of denying that they are brothers. At the supposedly last minute of his life, Chüeh-hui realizes how much he loves his brother and how much he has to say to him. Therefore, after his escape from death and before his departure for a remote place, Chüeh-hui assures his eldest brother of his fraternal love and urges him to live life more fully and more aggressively. For those who have lost freedom and experienced near death, Chüeh-hui tells his brother, life is so precious that every minute seems to contain endless happiness. Life thus is not to be wasted or sacrificed for icons or systems.

From his love for Ming-feng, his brothers, and other innocent and suffering members of his family, it is but another step for Chüeh-hui to broaden his love to embrace a whole segment of society and mankind. Like a self-proclaimed messiah, he is determined to define his own truth, propagate his own value system, and pave the way for others to attain happiness. Whether others can be made happy is another question; he will attempt to destroy those systems that have made others unhappy.

Chüeh-hui's struggle and vigorous rebellion contrast sharply with his eldest brother's submission and inertia. Until Chüeh-hui leaves the family, both brothers have undergone the same sufferings under the same socio-familial conditions. Afterwards, their lives and fortunes are understood to be diametrically different: the one who remains at home and adheres to the

old way of life will continue to suffer and pine away, while
the other will create an opportunity for a better life not only
for himself but for his fellow countrymen. Such a polarization
of choices and consequences is an old device with Ts'ao Yü: in
Sunrise, Fang Ta-sheng decides to struggle against Chin Pa
and survives, while Ch'en Pai-lu stays and dies; in *Peking Man,*
Tseng Wen-ch'ing returns home only to commit suicide, while
Su-fang leaves the house for a broad, new world.

At the end of *Family,* Chüeh-hsin, however, does not die,
but only suffers the loss of his wife. This variation gives the
play a poignancy unlike that in the earlier works. Previously,
Ming-feng has quoted Jui-chüeh as saying that to love a man
is to pave his way to happiness; in the resolution, Jui-chüeh
testifies to her doctrine of love with her death. To save her
husband from the inevitable arguments that he has to make
to maintain her rights, Jui-chüeh, as has already been mentioned, volunteers to deliver her baby at a remote farmhouse
and is dying from lack of care. When her husband joins her
in her last moments on earth, she feels very sorry to die, not
for her own sake, but because she cannot take care of her
husband and children anymore. Like Chüeh-hui under the
firing squad, Jui-chüeh is so anxious to see her husband change
that she immediately endorses Chüeh-hui's message to his eldest
brother (brought by other visitors) and urges him to be resolute,
optimistic, and courageous. If Chüeh-hsin had followed the
advice given him by his brother on the night before, he might
have saved his wife. Her death is a punishment for his delay
and proves the message's validity.

Jui-chüeh never complains or despairs. With virtually her
last breath, she only voices nostalgia mingled with hope. It
was a warm spring day when she was married to Chüeh-hsin,
a complete stranger to her at that time. After the guests were
gone and they were left alone with each other in the bridal
chamber at night, husband and wife were so preoccupied with
their own thoughts and emotions that they did not exchange
a word for a long time. The silence was merely punctuated by
desultory cuckoo calls which, however, became increasingly
intoxicating and passionate as the newlyweds were drawn gradually to each other into the consummation of their marriage.
This has happened almost three years ago and now it is deep

in winter and a heavy snow is falling. Somehow, a farm boy, anxiously expecting the tidings of spring, is imitating cuckoo calls, reviving memories that have long been buried:

JUI: Chüeh-hsin, do you remember that during our bridal night, cuckoos were calling by the lake?
HSIN: Yes, I do. That was just the beginning of spring.
JUI: Yes, the beginning of spring.
HSIN: It is winter now.
JUI: But winter in time will come to an end.
SHU-CHEN: Eldest brother, see she has closed her eyes.
HSIN: Jui—
(*Everyone approaches the death bed. Outside, the cuckoo calls continue, desultory and mournful, while the snow is falling heavily.*)
(p. 262)

Thus, Jui-chüeh and Chüeh-hsin reach in a duet what Shelley has proclaimed in a solo: "If Winter comes, can Spring be far behind?" Their tone, however, is subdued, and Chüeh-hsin's attitude, in particular, is despondent. It is Chüeh-hui's vigorous voice that recalls Shelley's romantic declaration:

Be thou, Spirit fierce,
My spirit! Be thou me, impetuous one!
Drive my dead thoughts over the universe
Like withered leaves to quicken a new birth!
And, by the incantation of this verse,
Scatter, as from an unextinguished hearth
Ashes and sparks, my words among mankind![4]

Before Jui-chüeh dies, three of her relatives come to visit her: Shu-chen, Chüeh-min, and Ch'in. Throughout the play, a minor strand of incidents concerns Shu-chen's feet being bound by her mother, despite Chüeh-hui's objection that foot-binding is inhuman and foolish. Thus, Jui-chüeh is comforted to know from Shu-chen that her mother has decided not to bind her feet any more. Still more encouraging news comes from the other two visitors. The proposed marriage for Chüeh-min, over which his brothers have heatedly debated and because of which Chüeh-min has run away from home under Chüeh-hui's encouragement, has been voluntarily canceled by Master Kao shortly before his death. Now, over Jui-chüeh's deathbed, Ch'in tells her that her mother has promised to let her attend school with Chüeh-min. These young lovers thus can expect to get

married in time and not repeat the tragedy that Chüeh-hsin and
Mei have undergone. The happiness of the lovers and the
freedom that Shu-chen feels, presented side by side with Jui-
chüeh's death, vindicate Chüeh-hui's previous efforts and foreshadow his future success.

What the future will be and what new system will replace
the traditional one the play does not specify. Like many of
Ts'ao Yü's plays which deal with the problems of his age,
Family exposes the evils of the large feudalistic family system.
From another viewpoint, the play is a tragedy of youthful love
in which two noble-minded women die innocently. Content
and submissive almost by nature, Ming-feng and Jui-chüeh are
unaware of how deep their love is or how great their sacrifice
is. Selfless not only in action but in mind as well, female characters like these are plentiful in the traditional Chinese theater,
but have few counterparts in Western theater. In the traditional
Chinese theater, poetic justice is often rendered to such characters at the end, but in *Family* their misfortunes become the
mainspring of social protest. It is because of this combination
of the traditional and the modern that *Family* will probably
achieve a unique position in Chinese dramatic literature.

CHAPTER 9

The Bridge

DESPITE powerful intervention, Shen Chih-fu, general manager of the Mou-hua Steel Company, refuses to purchase coal and pig iron of substandard quality. He tries to convince Ho Hsiang-ju, new director of the Board of Trustees, of the importance of "industrial spirit," but the latter is more interested in Emmy Liang, an attractive girl, than in the company's business.

Shen Ch'eng-ts'an, son of Chih-fu and a capable engineer, proposes to Kuei Jung-hsi but is refused, because his girl friend wishes to continue her education in music. Though momentarily disappointed, Shen immediately diverts his attention to his new project and succeeds in producing tons of refined steel. Unfortunately, an accident happens in the process and Shen loses one arm. Deeply moved, Kuei Jung-hsi decides to give up her own education and marry him.

The quality of the coal and pig iron recommended by Ho Hsiang-ju proving to be substandard, Shen Chih-fu refuses to sign any contract for purchase. In retaliation, Ho reduces the loan that he has arranged for the financing of the steel company. Worse still, the government suddenly cancels its plan to construct a railroad and therefore rescinds its offer to buy products of refined steel from the company. Instead of being discouraged, Shen decides to dedicate all he has to maintaining the operation of his steel company. He will sell part of the refined steel to a bridge construction company until a better opportunity arises.

The original edition of *The Bridge*, published in 1945, is prefixed with a quotation from John Milton: "Give me the liberty to know, to utter, and argue freely according to conscience, above all liberties."[1] Less than three years afterwards, the Communists gained complete control of the Chinese mainland and Ts'ao Yü lost not only his freedom of speech, but lost also his freedom of silence. As his seemingly final voluntary

109

work, *The Bridge* contains Ts'ao Yü's last version of the Utopia for which he has searched since beginning his literary career in 1933. This version, ironically, suggests overthrowing the government in power, thus advancing the Communist cause and helping to put to an end his own literary odyssey.

Set in the Mou-hua Steel Company near a large inland city during World War II, *The Bridge* is primarily a study of China's industrialization. In the exposition, it is made clear that because of inflation and government price control, the company is deeply in debt. Ling Tou-kuang, former director of the company's Board of Trustees, is forced to resign his position to Ho Hsiang-ju, who immediately arranges a large loan to tide the company over the financial crisis. Though Ho's bad reputation casts doubts on the company's future, the devoted engineers, particularly Shen Chih-fu and his son Shen Ch'eng-ts'an, are eagerly preparing the first output of refined steel, which the government will buy for use in constructing a new railroad. At the end of the play, the engineers have succeeded in producing tons of refined steel good enough to meet international standards, but by that time the government has rescinded its decision to construct the railroad, and Ho Hsiang-ju has decided to reduce the arranged loan which the company desperately needs. In light of this reversal, *The Bridge* is primarily a story of frustrated hope and wasted energy.

The setback of these engineers is treated not merely as personal, but as involving, in the long run, the welfare of the whole country. At one point, Shen Chih-fu tells Ho Hsiang-ju: "Industrialization is not confined to modernizing our backward productive techniques; it also means that we must resolutely use the industrial spirit to transform our entire backward political, social, and economic systems."[2] In order to promote such an important transformation, the dedicated industrialists, whose factories in Shanghai have either been destroyed or occupied by the Japanese, have pooled their capital and talent to found the steel company. Their purpose, as revealed during a conversation between Ling Tou-kuang and Shen Chih-fu, is not personal profit, but to train a group of scientists and engineers, to spread modern technical skill, to give others knowledge of industrial management, and thus to provide a foundation for China's industrial development.

The struggle of these dedicated men, furthermore, is presented as a rare opportunity for China to make the needed transition toward industrialization. From experience, these industrialists know how hard it is for an emerging industry to compete with more advanced industry. The Japanese wartime blockade temporarily shields China from foreign imports and provides the emerging Chinese industry a chance to mature free from this stifling competition. Shen Chih-fu and others are thus anxious to build a solid foundation for Chinese industry so that it may continue to compete and develop in peacetime.

The major conflict in the play is between a group of dedicated industrialists struggling to develop Chinese industry and a group of selfish entrepreneurs who oppose or sabotage this development. In the character sketch included in the play and in the dramatic action, Ho Hsiang-ju is presented as a man of tremendous influence in government and over such civilian enterprises as banks and transportation. Cabinet ministers are his close friends; some of them may have been his subordinates when he was in government service. Though he does not now hold any government position, he still has such strong influence that even the central national bank and the ministry of national finance stretch their policies in order to benefit his business. Unfortunately, Ho does not want to use this influence to develop an enterprise that is advantageous both to himself and to his country. His influence is not only wasted, it becomes a handicap to the development of free enterprise, for he can also misuse his government connection to smother honest business. The major conflict thus pits high government authorities and dishonest entrepreneurs against honest and dedicated industrialists.

Against such a perspective, *The Bridge* is more significant and appealing than it appears at first glance. The same conflict and problem presented in the play must be faced, sooner or later, by any underdeveloped country undergoing industrialization. The emerging industry will inevitably encounter strong competition from more advanced industrial countries, which *The Bridge* touches upon briefly, as well as domestic difficulties arising from differences of opinion among entrepreneurs and government officials. The political and economic situations in South America for example, reflect such crises. *The Bridge* suggests that these crises cannot be solved until governments which practice favoritism and cronyism are overthrown. Later political changes in China prove Ts'ao Yü's insight.

This insight is embodied in three closely intertwined actions. The first centers around Ho Hsiang-ju who, as a new director of the Board of Trustees, comes to inspect the company. The second shows the heroic struggle of Shen Chih-ju and his son to maintain and improve the steel company. The third concerns a love affair between Shen Ch'eng-ts'an and Kuei Jung-hsi.

According to Shen Chih-fu, the most fundamental problem facing the company is the lack of industrial spirit—a willingness to forgo favoritism for the sake of efficiency. Events in the play show that this spirit is exactly what Ho Hsiang-ju does not have. In the beginning of the play, he keeps the manager and chief engineer waiting for hours merely out of inexcusable tardiness. Later, he wants to dismiss the assistant I Fan-ch'i because the latter in the past criticized him in the newspapers. Worse still, he wants the company to buy coal and pig iron from companies under his patronage, even though their materials are of poor quality. In order to soften his resistance, Ho even tries to bribe Shen by presenting an estate to Shen's mother as a birthday gift. When neither coercion nor bribery works, he reduces (in an underhanded manner) the loan that he has arranged for the company. Even more damaging, he makes no use of his influence to reverse the government's decision to cancel the construction of the railway which has been the impetus for the company to improve its steel refining processes. In short, he controls the steel company, but he lacks the spirit essential for industrial development in a backward country.

In addition to his lack of industrial spirit, the play provides two incidents which illuminate why Ho Hsiang-ju prefers dishonest dealings. One is his illicit love affair with Emmy Liang, an attractive young lady, who favors Ho merely for his money and the privileges offered her by his friends and subordinates. The other involves the coal company whose salesman, Yang Wei-chai, bribes Ho's secretary so that the latter will force the steel company manager to purchase the poor-quality coal at a high price. Ho is not shown taking bribes, but by allowing his subordinates to exploit their favorable situation, he commands their loyalty and submission only through such favoritism. Instead of having the proper industrial spirit, Ho protects those

closest to him at the expense of the company and, in the long
run, of the entire country. In simplest terms, dishonesty can
bring him more privileges and profit than can honesty.

In contrast, the dedicated industrialists live an austere life,
work hard, and sometimes risk their lives for their ideals. The
second major strand of events reveal exactly how these industrialists live, work, and make sacrifices.

A recipient of a Ph.D. degree from the Carnegie Institute
of Technology, Shen Ch'eng-ts'an has not only obtained up-to-
date technical knowledge in his field, he also knows how to
adapt his knowledge to fit the actual situation in which he
works. He knows that the Bessemer process is an obsolete
method of refining steel, but, since the materials available to
him will not permit any other method, he brushes aside his
colleagues' criticism and supervises the construction of a Bessemer converter and other auxiliary equipment.

His success at producing tons of refined steel that can meet
international standards demonstrates that China has the talent
and materials to develop its own heavy industry. This success
results not only from his knowledge and perseverance, but from
a last-minute heroic sacrifice as well. The first output of the
Bessemer converter is endangered by an accident which threatens
to put an end to the whole attempt to refine steel. In an effort
to save the output, Shen Ch'eng-ts'an is so seriously injured
that one arm must be amputated. If his success can pave the
way for the company's expansion and, in the long run, China's
industrialization, he feels that his sacrifice is worth making.
But while he is waiting for the amputation, the news that the
government has decided not to build the railway reaches him.
The Bridge is thus a lamentation for wasted effort and sacrifice,
as well as a protest against the government and its favorite
entrepreneur, Ho Hsiang-ju.

Appropriately, a German-trained engineer curses the government decision. The scene then proceeds as follows:

SHEN CH'ENG-TS'AN (*stunned by the news, and then*): Papa, is
it true?

SHEN CHIH-FU (*heavy-hearted*): Yes, I have known it for two
days, but I did not tell you immediately, because I was afraid it
might affect you too much emotionally. This is certainly a bolt from
the blue! We have worked so hard and produced steel under such

difficult conditions, yet he [unspecified; most probably Ho Hsiang-ju]
would give us such an attack! But I don't believe this blow is fatal.
Now that we have waded through more than half of the muddy
water, there is no reason to retreat. During the past two days, I have
been contacting a bridge company for a long-term contract.

SHEN CH'ENG-TS'AN: But papa, bridge—

SHEN CHIH-FU: Yes, bridges won't use as much steel. But we
have to rely on these bridges to tide us over this hard time. Gradually,
we will find our way and a new market. I don't believe that for the
construction of a new China, during the wartime, twenty thousand
tons of steel produced by civilian companies will be sufficient.

Since the promised loan has been reduced from eighty million
dollars to thirty million, Shen Chih-fu decides to invest all his
personal capital in the company and to struggle on to the
very end.

In view of the overwhelmingly pernicious political, social,
and economic circumstances, the ultimate outcome of Shen
Chih-fu's struggle is, to say the least, doubtful. Through industrialization he expects to transform and modernize the backward
political, social, and economic systems of his country. Yet these
systems threaten to smother the development of heavy industry
even in its embryo. The guiding forces of these systems, the
leaders in government and society as personified in Ho Hsiang-ju,
Yang Wei-chai, or even I Fan-ch'i, are not by nature opposed
to industrialization. But their selfish and nest-feathering activities
create a well-nigh insurmountable obstacle to the development
of free enterprise and heavy industry.

In view of this obstacle, Shen Chih-fu's words are either
overly optimistic or symbolic. Symbolically, the bridge is a
device through which the steel company will overcome its
difficulties, prosper, and contribute proudly to the construction
of a new China. Will the construction start with the old government in power? By relying "on these bridges to tide us over
this hard time," does Shen Chih-fu imply that he is expecting
an easy time when Ho Hsiang-ju is removed from his influential
position? In that case, how can Ho be removed if those who
trust and empower him continue to hold their supreme positions?
Whatever the answers may be, the very questions that *The
Bridge* has raised could not help but disturb the government
in power.

On the surface, the third strand of action is merely a love

affair between Shen Ch'eng-ts'an and Kuei Jung-hsi, but actually it is closely entwined with the other two strands. In Act One, Kuei Jung-hsi rejects Shen's proposal in order to pursue her study of music. In Act Two, deeply moved by Shen's heroic sacrifice, Kuei Jung-hsi now promptly decides to marry him. Her reversal of decision gives him great joy and encouragement in a moment of great despair. It also magnifies the admiration due a selfless warrior dedicated to the cause of his country's industrialization and modernization. In contrast, Ho's failure to recognize and promote such a cause is made to appear even more inhumane and detestable.

The devoted but unrequited love that Emmy Liang bears for Shen Ch'eng-ts'an further clarifies the attitude of the play-wright. Shen's ability, appearance, and their childhood associ-ation account for a great deal of her affection for him. Yet Ho Hsiang-ju's money, position, and powerful connections ad-vance his relationship with this bold and attractive girl. He has obviously possessed her body more than once, but he has never won her respect or caused her heartfelt love for Shen Ch'eng-ts'an to weaken. Theirs is not really a true triangular love affair, but Emmy's attitude provides another barometer to indicate the allocation of respect and contempt, sympathy and antipathy, love and hatred in the play.

The Bridge contrasts interestingly with *Metamorphosis,* and in many ways they serve to counterpoint each other in Ts'ao Yü's symphony of wartime plays. Both plays advocate organi-zational and attitudinal changes as a prelude to China's self-salvation and modernization. In the earlier play the changes are successfully introduced through the efforts of Inspector Liang, and consequently the hospital functions effectively. In *The Bridge,* Shen Chih-fu advocates the faithful observation of an industrial spirit in the steel company, but his boss Ho Hsiang-ju is incorrigible, and the steel company suffers a severe setback. In these contradictory results, Ts'ao Yü has demon-strated both sides of the coin: change leading to prosperity, and stagnation leading to decline.

If Ho Hsiang-ju were as enlightened and as dedicated as Inspector Liang, the steel company under his supervision would certainly thrive, for the scientists and engineers in *The Bridge* are as competent and conscientious in their work as Dr. Ting is in her medical service. Leadership makes the difference. Dr. Ting can only protest and then resign before the inspector arrives to overhaul the hospital organization and dismiss the incompetent officials. Likewise, Shen Chih-fu and Shen Ch'eng-ts'an can accomplish little under their incompetent and selfish director of the Board of Trustees; but there is no authority to dismiss Ho Hsiang-ju, who has connections in the highest government circles and is sometimes a part of them.

The ideas embodied in *The Bridge* show a remarkable advance over those in Ts'ao Yü's earliest social problem play, *Sunrise*. Instead of a vague diagnosis of the malady of Chinese society and an embittered indictment of an unseen Chin Pa, *The Bridge* pins down the ultimate source of China's illness. Instead of placing all hope in the laborers as the future of China, *The Bridge* now presents a more balanced view in which well-educated scientists and untrained laborers work together. In contrast to Fang Ta-sheng's announcement that he will do something against Chin Pa or for The Shrimp, Shen Chih-fu and his son dedicate themselves to the cause of industrialization and hardly raise a voice of protest. Fang Ta-sheng represents Ts'ao Yü at the early phase of his dramatic career when he was outraged by the illnesses of his society and country; Shen Chih-fu and Shen Ch'eng-ts'an represent a mature Ts'ao Yü who can now prescribe a cure.

In techniques, *Sunrise* reveals its author's anxiety to convince his audience. Consequently, characters and events tend toward the extreme: a villainous Chin Pa and suicides of the most pathetic nature. In comparison, *The Bridge* shows an author confident of his art and assured of the correctness of his thought. He thus can afford to have humorous touches in intense moments and touches of genuinely romantic love in the midst of despair and pathos. More important, the protest is only implied; the iconoclastic implication is only suggested by the events themselves, not through direct arguments and vehement speeches. As a consequence, the tone is subdued, the tempo is relaxed, and the emotions it arouses are less extreme. All these, in addition to the fact that *The Bridge* involves too many technical details about the Bessemer process of refining steel, make the play less popular than *Sunrise*.[3] But for analytical minds, *The Bridge* offers many mature ideas for reflection.

CHAPTER 10

Bright Skies

WHILE Peking is surrounded by the Communists, Mrs. Chao Shu-te arrives at the Peking Union Medical College for treatment of her rickets. Dr. Jackson, the Director, assigns Dr. Sun Jung to handle the case. Meanwhile, despite the great turmoil caused by the siege, Dr. Ling Shih-hsiang continues his research on the law governing the dissemination of plague.

After the Communist takeover, the son of Mrs. Chao Shu-te complains to the Communist director of the hospital about her suspicious death. The Communist director asserts that Dr. Jackson has murdered his patient and promises to investigate so that the philanthropic image of American doctors in China will be repudiated.

More than two years pass without bringing to light any evidence. Meanwhile, the Korean war breaks out. Dr. Ling is told that the Americans, benefited by his findings about the law governing the dissemination of plague that he published in a journal in the United States, have conducted germ warfare in Korea. After he sees an exhibition of materials collected on the front, Dr. Ling is fully convinced of the American crime and volunteers to work in Korea.

Just before his departure, the case involving Mrs. Chao also comes to a head. Confronted by witnesses and material evidence produced by the Communists, Dr. Sun Jung confesses that he, under the direction of Dr. Jackson, has indeed murdered Mrs. Chao. From these personal experiences, Dr. Ling realizes how important it is to follow the guidance of the Communist Party and to distinguish between people's scientists and the imperialists' scientists.

As noted earlier,[1] though *Bright Skies* is published under Ts'ao Yü's name, it is most likely not a voluntary production. At the very least, the play appears to have been tinkered with by politicians who unfortunately are literary amateurs. Thus, one must be cautious in basing an evaluation of Ts'ao Yü's art and thought on it.[2] On the other hand, defective and dull as the play is, it is revealing of the Communist society under which it was written just as Ts'ao Yü's earlier works are revealing of Nationalist society. With this background in mind, the play itself can be better understood.

Set in the famous Peking Union Medical College, formerly financed by the Rockefeller Foundation, the dramatic action begins on the eve of the Communist takeover and ends when the Korean War is at its most intense stage. The protagonist is Dr. Ling Shih-hsiang, professor of bacteriology at the college, through whose change in thought and action the play attempts to demonstrate that intellectuals must undergo thought reform under the guidance of the Communist Party. At the beginning of the play, Dr. Ling is shown as a scientist totally absorbed in his research; at the end, he volunteers to work at the Korean front. This reversal is brought about by two important discoveries, the development of which occupies most of the play.

The rest of the incidents are only loosely related to the main action; they involve politicians who slander the Nationalists and praise the Communists. One of these incidents shows a Kuomintang aide-de-camp desperately begging a physician to examine his commander's wife, only to discover that she has already left out of fear of the approaching Communists without bothering to notify him. Another scene shows some Kuomintang plainclothesmen avidly collecting personal properties from suspected Communist underground workers. After the Communist takeover, one incident involves a political commissar who is hospitalized for an eye injury suffered at the Korean front. Though the loss of his eyesight is imminent following failure of an operation, this exemplary Communist zealously continues his political work from his sickbed. While the propaganda value of these scenes is dubious, their inclusion certainly disrupts the development of major lines of action.

In the first of the major lines of action, Dr. Jackson, former head of the medical college, an American, is accused of having ruthlessly murdered Mrs. Chao, wife of a Chinese factory worker and a victim of rickets, in order to procure her bones as pathological specimens. In the second line of action, the United States is accused of conducting germ warfare in Korea.

In the beginning, Dr. Ling is suspicious of these charges, but eventually comes to believe them. It is through his conversion that indoctrination and propaganda are attempted; but it is through the manipulation of his conversion that the obnoxious nature of thought reform is inadvertently exposed.

Of the two main lines of action, the one concerning germ warfare may be dealt with first, since it is less integral. The subject of germ warfare is not introduced until the end of Act Two, Scene One, when Director Tung of the hospital invites Dr. Ling Shih-hsiang to participate in a meeting of a committee preparing an exhibition on germ warfare. Though doubtful that American bacteriologists would degrade themselves by participaitng in germ warfare, Dr. Ling agrees to take a look at the exhibition. In the next scene, which takes place three days later, throughout which the audience is asked to believe that he has been at the exhibition constantly, he returns a crushed man. When asked by Chiang Tao-tsung, a pro-American professor, "Is it because of the anti-germ warfare...," he interrupts Chiang rudely, saying, "There is germ warfare."[3] With this curt assertion, the act closes, giving no clue as to how Dr. Ling has made such a discovery. Even though the audience is thus left in the dark and remains unconvinced, this discovery proves that Dr. Ling's attitudes and succeeding action will be drastically altered.

A day has passed when, in the next scene he informs Director Tung that he has already decided to organize an anti-germ warfare team to work in Korea. A fortnight later, while packing for the Korean front, he talks with his daughter: "Last night, the exhibition committee received new material from the Northeast Front. What do you think I saw? Moles!—dropped by the American imperialists from airplanes. This kind of mole does not ordinarily carry the plague; but all these air-dropped moles do! Do you know who discovered the laws governing moles' susceptibility to the plague?" (p. 108). He is referring to his own paper, published three years before in an American scientific journal, and his subsequent cooperation with American scientists on research about the suceptibility of moles to plague.

This practically exhausts the subject of germ warfare. Though short and naive like one of Æsop's fables, it includes some rather tumid moral lessons. Apart from some of the most ap-

parent and odious ones, the story is supposed to sustain the
argument that scientific cooperation with the U.S. must be
severed. In Communist terminology, a demarcation line must
be drawn between the people's scientists and the imperialists'
scientists.

Considerably more attention is devoted to those scenes concerning Dr. Jackson's atrocious murder of a Chinese woman;
this accusation suffers from overexposure. As in a lawsuit, the
play presents the defendant and prosecutor, the victim and her
next of kin, eyewitnesses and material evidence. The procedures,
however, are those of a political trial presented under the
guise of an objective and righteous search for equity and justice.
It is not until near the end of the play that the political
prosecutors are able to present any real evidence, although the
verdict has been reached in Act One. Obviously, the intervening
three years become merely a period for collecting and fabricating
evidence to support an unalterable political conclusion.

The case in question involves the sudden death of Mrs. Chao
Shu-te, wife of a factory worker, while under the treatment
of Dr. Sun Yung in the medical college's hospital. Approximately
ten months later, after the hospital has been transferred to the
Communists, her son complains to the new director: "Director
Tung, last year we took my mother to this very room. Strangely,
my mother disappeared; not even her corpse has been seen"
(p. 39). Though the record of Mrs. Chao's treatment appears
to be faultless, Ling Mu-lan jumps to a conclusion: "We feel
this is the fiendish trick of Jackson, who used this patient for
his rickets experiment" (p. 40).

Two years pass without bringing to light any shred of evidence, but the speculators grow more instead of less firm in
their conviction that Jackson is guilty. Dr. Sun has been put
under increasing pressure to confess that he has fraudulently
altered the record of the case; and though he has denied this
with tears in his eyes, he is not believed. As long as he refuses
to confess, he is systematically alienated from his colleagues,
required to appear at long drawn-out meetings, and subjected
to various other kinds of mental torture. Once he confesses
his guilt, he is surprisingly not only forgiven, but is received
with warmth by his "progressive" colleagues. In his own words:

I suffered for three years. Last night, during the meeting of the interior department, I told my colleagues everything. Far from rejecting me, they welcomed me and encouraged me. I have never received such a profound education.   (p. 112)

While Dr. Sun's self-incriminating confession has freed him from the protracted suffering of three years, it serves also to incriminate Dr. Jackson, under whose direction and for whose experiments Mrs. Chao Shu-te was supposedly murdered. It does not matter that the former director of the medical college and hospital has returned to the United States and is thus beyond the jurisdiction of Peking; what really counts is that once his guilt is pronounced, his previous reputation as a humanitarian scientist and altruistic educator is totally demolished. This, the eradication of veneration for America as a prelude to the elimination of American influence, is the real purpose of the whole sequence involving the murder charge. This purpose is not only undisguised, it is elaborated upon in an early stage of the action:

DIRECTOR TUNG: Let's sit down and talk. Comrade T'ieh-sheng, the murderer of your mother is not Sun Yung, but the American doctor named Jackson who tricked your mother into the hospital. He hid behind the scenes all the time, using Dr. Sun as a front. But everything was arranged by that Jackson! That murderer Jackson had returned to the United States before we came.

CHAO T'IEH-SHENG: Director Tung, are we then going to give up?

DIRECTOR TUNG: By no means. Our people should not have died in vain. We must clarify the matter through investigation. But here is the problem: as you know, the record of the case is flawless. Only Dr. Sun knows the hidden truth.

. . . .

Comrade T'ieh-sheng, we must ask him to tell the whole truth, and through him, let everybody know who is the murderer of your mother. But this takes time and requires educational work on ideology. Yet, when one day everybody knows the truth, the doctors in the hospital will see clearly that Jackson is a cultural spy of the United States. We will then find our true enemy and launch our attack.
                                                             (pp. 55-56)

As has been mentioned earlier, the accusation against Dr. Sun begins in 1949 and drags on for three years without any progress. Act Two, Scene I, opens on a day in July, 1952, with a stage direction outlining the tremendous changes that have taken place: "Particularly during the recent one and a half year's resist-America-assist-Korea Campaign, everybody seems to have been considering one question: who are our enemies, and who are our own men?" (pp. 59-60). The microcosmic world of the medical college hospital keeps pace with the nation at large and undergoes convulsive changes in the eventful month of July. A Nurse Chien, suddenly remembered and located by the relentless cadres, testifies that Dr. Jackson used lice to contaminate Mrs. Chao with typhus. Dr. Sun is thus compelled to admit that the record of the patient has indeed been changed: Mrs. Chao died of typhus instead of pneumonia, as the record has stated. The box which contained her bones and which was moved from the hospital to Chiang Tao-tsung's house by a servant is also uncovered when the servant suddenly realizes what the box must be. Furthermore, Jackson's secretary, Mary Liu, revealed to be an American spy, testifies that Dr. Jackson was collecting information for the U.S. Department of State. It would be tedious to go into all the contradictions and farfetched arguments of these developments; suffice it to say that the very multiplicity of them in so short a time renders them incredible. For when arrows shower upon a target from divergent sources and in quick succession, the presence of a signaler is suggested.

The signaler in this case is Director Tung Kuan-shan, who is carrying out the Party's directives to effectuate thought reform among intellectuals working in a once prestigious, American financed medical institute. He is comparable to Inspector Liang in *Metamorphosis*, who also is entrusted by the central government with conducting necessary institutional and attitudinal reforms in a wartime hospital. But whereas Inspector Liang sometimes radiates personal warmth, sometimes bursts into indignation over corruption and inefficiency, and always is frank and lovable, Director Tung appears enigmatic in his intentions and devious in his dealings with his subordinates. Except for the occasion upon which he explains the necessity of thought reform, he is cryptic in speech, choosing to lurk behind the scenes while pulling the strings. He is a manipulator, tinkering with intellectuals' brains, whereas Inspector Liang is a reformer, sonorously calling for battle against the corrupted layers in man's mind and in society. Moreover, Inspector Liang

is the model new Chinese official dedicated to the construction
of an ideal country, whereas Director Tung is a Communist
bureaucrat working for a police state which claims already to
be ideal. Finally, Inspector Liang is the creation of Ts'ao Yü's
flamboyant aspiration and enthusiasm, whereas Director Tung
is an unwelcome child whose parent is ashamed of him and
who tries to disclaim him.

A parallel situation is to be found in the delineation of
Dr. Ling, the protagonist of *Bright Skies,* and Dr. Ting, the
protagonist of *Metamorphosis.* Both are devoted medical scientists who have received their education in the United States;
both enjoy great renown for their integrity as well as for their
knowledge; similarly, while Dr. Ting is a widow with a grown-up
son, Dr. Ling is a widower with an adult daughter. Other
similar personality traits can be seen by comparing the character
sketches included in stage directions, but all these similarities
only serve to emphasize the political circumstances which sur-
round them and demand different behavioral patterns from
them; as a result, the impact of the two plays is immensely
different. Or, to look at the matter from a different perspective,
because of the similarities in personal background and inclin-
ation, Dr. Ling and Dr. Ting potentially may follow a similar
behavioral pattern, but because of the different dramatic situations, their actual behavior diverges considerably. This difference in dramatic situations stems largely from the political
circumstances under which the characters live and work. Consequently, the influence of these political circumstances on the
protagonists is worth pursuing.

The nature of the imaginary world embodied in the action
is symbolically indicated in the titles of the plays. *Metamorphosis*
implies the existence of certain undesirable elements which are
to be shed during the process of drastic change. Dr. Ting is
unsparing and fearless in her condemnation of such undesirable
elements as corruption and nepotism. *Bright Skies,* the title
of which is taken from a dialogue in which the arrival of the
Communists is compared to the clearing up of overcast skies
(p. 36), eulogizes Communist rule which is said to be as spotless
as never-ending sunshine. Any disparagement is thus tantamount
to staining the reputation of an enlightened government. Thus,
even though Dr. Ling is endowed by his creator with the same

tenacious aversion to vice and falsehood as Dr. Ting, he is
never permitted to utter any straightforward condemnation of
Communist policy. Disgusting as the accusation against Dr. Jackson and Dr. Sun is to him, at least in its early phase, Dr. Ling can
only murmur a qualified protest. Thus, whereas Dr. Ting often
bursts into outraged and eloquent speeches, regardless of her
efforts to control herself, Dr. Ling's speeches are characteristically muffled and guarded, often ending with a puzzled moan.
For example, he says to Director Tung meditatively:

Perhaps I am really getting old. My thoughts are indeed confused.
But, Director Tung, I really cannot imagine a bacteriologist engaged
in germ warfare, just as I cannot imagine Jackson would murder
people.   (p. 71)

As for the parent-child relationship, the warmth and mutual
affection between mother and son in *Metamorphosis* and the
lukewarm, indifferent, and even slightly hostile relationship
between Dr. Ling and his daughter presents a striking contrast.
It is understandable that strife is inevitable since Ling Mu-lan
is one of the most active of the thought reformers and her
father one of the old doctors needing reform. But one cannot
help wondering whether it is Ts'ao Yü's negligence or the
demand of the situation when Ling Mu-lan, after causing
her father great concern by an absence of three days, answers
her inquisitive father with a couple of cryptic sentences before
going away to see her boy friend. If blood relatives treat each
other like this, relations among colleagues and friends can
hardly be much better. As a result, the atmosphere in *Bright
Skies* is chilly, depressing, and ominous, like a cloudy winter
morning.

With an atmosphere so cold and overcast, with a protagonist
who rapidly loses his confidence and finally confesses his error,
with the speeches of all characters marked by constraint and
curtness, and with two major incidents lacking in plausibility,
Bright Skies has little to recommend it. It is a bad play. It is,
as many critics have pointed out, a dull play. Yet, *Bright Skies*
is significant in that it serves as a barometer of the political
atmosphere in Peking, of the worries and concerns of China's
new leaders, and of the methods through which they seek
to achieve their ends.

CHAPTER 11

The Gall and the Sword

IN 492 B.C., King Kou-chien of Yüeh is captured by King Fu-ch'a of Wu. In order to demonstrate his generosity to other kings and dukes, Fu-ch'a not only spares Kou-chien; he also releases the Yüeh king after three years of imprisonment.

Never for a moment does Fu-ch'a forget his defeat, and, for nineteen years, he has his people work hard for the recovery of their independence and national pride. The Wu army intervenes constantly, but through brilliant strategy and heroic sacrifices, Yüeh is able to circumvent its conquerors.

Finally, in 473 B.C., Yüeh launches an attack against Wu, captures King Fu-ch'a, and immediately puts him to death.

The Gall and the Sword was first published in *People's Literature* in the combined issues of July and August, 1961. Though two minor writers are named as collaborators, the actual writing is specifically attributed to Ts'ao Yü.

The Gall and the Sword is a historical play based on a variety of sources which deal with the protracted struggles between the kingdoms of Wu and Yüeh during the fifth century B.C. During this age of decline for the Chou dynasty, which had reigned in China since the last decade of the twelfth century B.C., local princes claimed royal titles and prerogatives and waged incessant wars of expansion and supremacy. In order to reestablish peace and order, Confucius (551-479 B.C.) advocated restoration of authority to the old royal house, but his words went unheeded. His disciple Mencius (372?-289 B.C.), moved by the wide devastation caused by the wars, categorically condemned the ambitious princes as unjust and immoral.[1]

The wars between Wu and Yüeh, if treated as a series of self-perpetuating struggles of rulers, would deserve condemnation; but traditionally and in the present play the story is not treated in this way. Although there was a feud between the ruling houses of Wu and Yüeh, the struggles which began in

492 B.C. and which *The Gall and the Sword* treat, can be and
have long been interpreted as the resolute campaign of a
subjugated nation to achieve freedom and independence. In
492 B.C., the army of Yüeh was defeated, its king, Kou-chien,
captured, and its people subjugated. For two decades, Kou-
chien and his people suffered under the domination of an alien
ruler; nevertheless, they never relaxed their preparations, made
in great secrecy and by shrewd maneuvering, for a decisive
battle of liberation. The opportunity finally came in 473 B.C.,
when, with brilliant diplomatic and military strategies, the
army of Yüeh captured the capital of its archenemy, forced the
king of Wu, Fu-ch'a, to commit suicide, and restored pride and
independence to its own people.

Using this interpretation, the Wu-Yüeh struggles can readily
serve to embody the idea that, through incessant and concerted
efforts, even a weak and conquered nation can eventually prevail. It is precisely for its potential to encourage a modern
audience that this interpretation is used in *The Gall and the
Sword*. In an article published in 1961, T'ien Han, an eminent
playwright and a high-ranking official in the Ministry of Culture, states:

Because the Party urged assiduity and frugality in the cause for
national construction and self-sufficiency, many writers have sought
successful precedence in historical figures such as Emperor T'ai-tsung
of T'ang and King Kou-chien of Yüeh. The latter, in particular, is a
ready-made protagonist, since to remind him of his humiliating
defeat, he volunteered to suffer the ordeals of sleeping on firewood
at night and tasting bitter gall while awake. Consequently, eighty
to ninety plays with him as the protagonist have appeared in various
regions in a short period [1958-1961].[2]

Mao Tun, then Minister of Culture, estimated in 1962 that
more than one hundred historical plays about the Wu-Yüeh
wars had appeared in the preceding four years.[3] On the basis
of the fifty-odd plays that he had read, he asserted that Ts'ao
Yü's *The Gall and the Sword* was the only one in spoken-drama
form and that it was the best of all the plays based on this story.[4]

Divided into five acts, *The Gall and the Sword* opens in
492 B.C. after the army of Yüeh has been defeated and its king
captured; it ends in 473 B.C. when Yüeh sends King Fu-ch'a
of Wu to his death and regains its freedom and independence.

The dramatic action, which occurs over this twenty-year period, unfolds a series of strategies by which the captured king of Yüeh gains his release, returns to his country and consolidates his people, increases the population and food supplies, manufactures and accumulates a supply of arms, and builds a naval power. Finally, with the aid of its allies, Yüeh launches the attack that brings victory.

Although the action of the play is extremely extensive in scope and poses a great dramaturgical challenge, Ts'ao Yü has managed to give it coherence and clarity. The techniques include judicious selection of events and delicate employment of vivid images. In the presentation of the events, Ts'ao Yü consistently stresses those crucial moments in which the various strategies are decided upon, sidestepping the complications involved in their execution. As a result, depth of thought embodied in pregnant and precise language becomes a major attraction of the play. A few examples can serve as illustrations, and, at the same time, show how the action is developed.

After the King of Yüeh is captured, Wu Tzu-hsü, a loyal but headstrong general of Wu, ponders the danger that a reprieve for the enemy king may create:

Auspice and portent, blessing and disaster are cognate. Auspice is often the beginning of portent, while a blessing frequently entails disasters. If we fail to eliminate this dangerous prisoner promptly, our glorious victory today may become the fountainhead of catastrophe in the future. Oh, how frightened I feel![5]

Thus, General Wu places national security above all else, but Minister Po-hsi, knowing that his own king is interested in expanding his territories still further, points out the possible international repercussions of executing a captured king:

My liege, I have heard that the dignity of a great man will never be hurt by the stings of ants and mosquitoes. Kou-chien has indeed been very impertinent and unreasonable, but should you spare him, the more your benevolence will shine, and the sooner the world will submit to you in heart.   (p. 21)

Consequently, in order to demonstrate his generosity, the ambitious king of Wu not only spares his royal prisoner but releases Kou-chien after three years' imprisonment. Before Kou-chien's release, however, Wu asks that, in exchange, Yüeh

disband its active guerrilla army of five thousand strong. When
Yüeh's minister Fan-li reports to Kou-chien that he has declined
to make such a definite promise, his queen is surprised and
disturbed. Fan-li explains:

My dear queen, we would have been trapped in making any such
promise. Po-hsi would then proclaim the promise to disband the
five thousand guerrillas throughout our country, and our liege would
forfeit the loyalty of his people even before his return. In the second
place, our promise would be tantamount to admitting that our liege
has secret connections with the guerrillas even though he is in prison.
Wu Tzu-hsü would then find a substantial reason to have His
Majesty killed.   (p. 31)

After his release, the King of Yüeh immediately initiates a
series of national recovery programs, but not without difficulty.
As soon as Yüeh has completed a wall around its capital, for
example, the Wu occupation army demands that it be leveled
to the ground. To refuse the demand would mean open defiance
and war, but to submit would lower morale and cause civil
disobedience. Minister Fan-li suggests a compromise: to remove
all the gates. When his king wrathfully upbraids him for such
a seemingly nonresistant policy, Minister Fan-li explains:

Death may precede life, while destruction may pave the way for
construction. Analogously, when an army is shown that there is no
retreat, it may fight the battle out and survive. Now, to remove the
gates will dispel the King of Wu's suspicion and make him no longer
regard us as a thorn in his eye. To remove the gates will also remind
us that the Wu army may overrun us at any time and warn us not
to lead an easy life. My liege, a city wall functions only in defense,
but all our present efforts are made for offense in the future. If we
are content with retreat and think of advance no more, the small
area held by us is quite insufficient for self-preservation. In light of
this analysis, it is really insignificant whether we level the wall or
not.   (p. 59)

It is through speeches such as these that Ts'ao Yü has managed to present with clarity the reversal of fortune of two rival
nations. Other playwrights treating the same historical story
tend to curtail the activities of the courtiers and the people and
stress the King of Yüeh's determination for revenge and the
King of Wu's infatuation with a beautiful girl who is offered
to him by Yüeh. In some plays, the whole conflict is reduced

to the activity of a female spy, Hsi-shih. Of her, one dictionary records: "Hsi-shih: famous beauty during 5th century B.C. A daughter of humble parents in Cheking, she was taken and trained and afterwards used to debauch the prince of Wu and cause his defeat."[6] Ts'ao Yü uses this beauty only in one short episode, devoting major attention to other maneuvers without which the victory of a subjugated nation over its oppressors would seem impossible.

Even playwrights of great renown have shown a tendency to neglect or slight the social and economic factors which weigh heavily in the outcome of conflicts between nations or royal houses. They choose instead to emphasize the personal valor and wisdom of the leaders, especially those of the victorious side. As a consequence, national wars are often portrayed through cursory military skirmishes and political intrigues, while major attention is given to the events surrounding the central characters. Schiller's *Wilhelm Tell* and *Don Carlos* are conspicuous examples. Even Shakespeare's historical plays have a tendency to focus on individual characters, relegating the political and military events to the background. As Margaret Webster has observed:

From the very beginning, with his *Henry VI* collaboration, Shakespeare reserved the dramatist's right of selection; and, as he wrote them, he became increasingly absorbed in the presentation of character. By the time he reached the mature writing of the *Henry IV*'s he had realized that one Falstaff was worth more than a king's ransom, and that the Boar's Head tavern in Eastcheap was a more fruitful sphere of action than any field of battle he had yet encountered.[7]

To include significant factors involved in the reversal and yet to be cohesive in the unfolding of the action, *The Gall and the Sword* makes considerable use of the second device, the delicate use of images. Whereas the first device, deliberation about crucial strategies and policies, revolves around the kings, generals, and courtiers, the use of images is largely used in connection with the common people. Only through the vivid presentation of the sufferings and sacrifices of the common people, as suggested through imagery, does the play succeed in dispelling the impression that the Wu-Yüeh wars were merely a feud between the rulers of two countries and in conveying

the idea that they were actually a national struggle for the
benefit of the people. The influence of Communist ideology is
obvious but, as far as dramatic techniques are concerned, the
images are superbly adapted to the action.

The three most prominent and extended images are the gall,
the sword, and rice. The title of the play combines the first
two images. Since all three images are closely related to K'u-
ch'eng, his position in the action will be examined first. The
definition of K'u is "bitter; thus, sorrow, suffering; in bad circumstances; painstaking, earnest."[8] The definition of Ch'eng
is "to complete; to perfect; to succeed. To become finished."[9]
In view of the political atmosphere in which the play was
composed, K'u-ch'eng obviously signifies success through hardship or completion despite bad circumstances. Historically, K'u-
ch'eng was a high-ranking official who contributed little to
Yüeh's struggle and survived the king. In the play, he is characterized as a common peasant, with two grandsons, upon whom,
significantly, the King of Yüeh bestows names meaning Plough
and Sword.

The play opens with fire and smoke in the background; the
Wu army is burning rice stores and fields captured during a
battle. Later, a Yüeh peasant rushes in with a bundle of scorched
rice stalks which he intends to show to his king as evidence
of the conqueror's ruthlessness. He is killed by a Wu soldier
but, before he dies, he asks his daughter to pass on the rice
stalks to the king. When the little girl is unable to reach the
king, K'u-ch'eng takes them, elbows his way to the captured
king, and is wounded in one arm by the surrounding Wu
soldiers. With the other arm, however, he presents the rice
stalks to the departing king, saying: "My liege, don't forget
the Yüeh people and Yüeh land" (p. 26). The scorched rice
accompanies the king to his prison, recalls to his mind his
devastated kingdom and impoverished people, and stimulates
him to think of means of improving methods and tools of culti-
vation so as to increase production. Furthermore, since blood
has been shed again and again in the attempt to present him
with it, the scorched rice stands for the indomitable spirit of a
temporarily conquered nation.

After the king's release, a severe drought and the occupation
army cause a poor harvest and widespread famine. To relieve

his people of acute hunger and to win their goodwill, the king distributes to them the rice grains that the King of Wu has sent him for personal use, but the people reject the gift after they learn the original source of the supply. First infuriated, then humiliated but finally enlightened, Kou-chien happily admits his mistake and says: "Indeed, a nation without rice is not poor, a nation without ambition is" (p. 58). When he asks K'u-ch'eng and others how they cultivate their land, they tell him that when the cattle are taken or destroyed by the Wu army, they pull the ploughs themselves; and that when the ploughs are confiscated, they use their bare hands. Neither hostile interference nor natural catastrophes nor lack of tools can deter a resolute people in their struggle for self-sufficiency. Their effort is well paid. They have won their struggle in the paddy field long before they win victory on the battlefield and regain their independence.

In the first act, in a moment of wrath, the King of Wu thrusts his sword into a rock. Naming it Subduing Yüeh Holy Sword, he decrees death for whoever dares to touch it, along with all his relatives even of the most remote connection. Later, declaring that "the country of Yüeh cannot be subdued" (p. 26), K'u-ch'eng carries away the sword, keeps it for years, and presents it to his king after the latter has returned. Surprised but elated, the king ejaculates prophetically: "Good sword, someday you will prove very useful" (p. 61).

Wu's effort to recover the stolen sword gradually intensifies and culminates in a house-to-house search supervised by a special envoy from the Wu court. Caches of hidden weapons that the Yüeh government and people have accumulated for years are in danger of being exposed if the search continues. For a while there seems no better way of stopping the search than to surrender the object of the search. Yet to return the stolen sword would be a devastating blow to the people's morale as well as to the king's prestige. To rescue his country from this dilemma, K'u-ch'eng surrenders himself to the Wu envoy, misleadingly confesses that he has thrown the sword into the river, and then commits suicide. In his memory, the name of the place where K'u-ch'eng dies is subsequently changed to K'u-ch'eng Precipice.

An interval of fifteen years elapses before the next act opens, but there is hardly a lapse in the dramatic action, for the new act opens by the precipice and with K'u-ch'eng's fellow countrymen invoking his name and inviting his spirit to witness the progress made in every field since his death. The progress, indeed, is so frightening to Yüeh's enemies that Fu-ch'a feels it necessary to conduct a personal inspection before going to an international summit conference at which he expects to be awarded new titles and honors. When he asks about the Subduing Yüeh Holy Sword,[10] the King of Yüeh answers with a double entendre that he "certainly will return it before too long" (p. 107).

The sword is certainly given back to the King of Wu soon afterwards, but by then he has become a prisoner and the sword is now a tool with which to commit suicide. As may be seen, the sword as an image is used for multiple purposes. It bridges the gap of years and thus brings continuity to the development of the action; it vivifies the humiliation, resolution, and sacrifices of the Yüeh people; it foreshadows the dénouement; and, finally, it underlines the theme that an aggressor will be destroyed by his own sword, even in a literal sense.

Another major image is the gall. In *Historical Records,* it is recorded that after his release the King of Yüeh licked daily the bitter gall that hung by his throne, while asking himself the question: "Have you forgotten the shame of K'uai-chi?" (K'uai-chi was the name of his capital where he was defeated and captured.) Many Chinese medical books assert that the galls of animals improve human eyesight and mollify choleric temperament.[11] In the play, Ts'ao Yü eruditely combines these sources of information in the third of his major images, the gall or the gall bladder.

In compliance with Communist ideology, the King of Yüeh in the play is not characterized as a ruler of eminent valor or wisdom. He possesses resolution, but it goads him into choleric anger which might have aborted the national recovery, if his courtiers and people had not prevailed over him. To cure him of his hot temper and to impress on him that forbearance is as important as resolution in the discharge of his responsibility, K'u-ch'eng, just before he goes to the Wu army to sacrifice himself, presents a gallbladder to his king as a gift with the following advice: "The gall can brighten one's eyes and improve

one's eyesight. My liege, you must observe with clear vision"
(p. 82). He goes on to suggest that a lasting victory is based
on moral principles, not on sheer physical strength.

Though this moral platitude fails to alter the course of
action in any perceptible way, the effect of the advice is
profound and lasting. Especially after his ennobling death, K'u-
ch'eng's last words become his will and testament which the
King of Yüeh pledges to honor and fulfill. In a monologue of
more than two pages in length and broken only momentarily
by a guard's recurring question: "Kou-ch'eng, have you forgotten
the shame of K'uai-chi," the King of Yüeh muses over his
temperamental weakness, contemplates the trouble-laden future
of his country, and, drawing lessons and inspiration from the
gall and K'u-ch'eng, emerges with new resolutions to reform
himself and to redouble his efforts in the national struggle for
independence. Thus, the image of the gall is effectively used
to bring about an important development in the thought and
personality of a major character. Furthermore, by ascribing
the gall to K'u-ch'eng, instead of to the king himself, as recorded
in *Historical Records,* Ts'ao Yü is once more eulogizing the
common people by demonstrating that the intellectual caliber
of the proletariat is higher than that of their feudalistic ruler.

In light of the above examination, it is clear that the influence
of Communist ideology permeates the whole play from theme
to characterization, from the selection of incidents to the use
of imagery. But as far as structural techniques are concerned,
Ts'ao Yü has probably succeeded as well as any writer can
while complying with Communist ideology. Through the extensive employment of images he has achieved an impression of
rapid movement and sustained tension in the unfolding of the
dramatic action, though it actually covers a period of more
than twenty years. By presenting deliberations on the feasibility
of certain policies or rationales for strategies already taken, he
has been able to give a most succinct yet rather comprehensive
examination of the major events and causes in the reversal of
fortune of two hostile nations. Even in characterization, Ts'ao Yü
demonstrates rather sound judgment. Unlike some of his fellow
playwrights who have either ignored Kou-chien or made a
buffoon of him because he belonged to the feudalistic ruling
class, Ts'ao Yü has given Kou-chien the unassailable dignity

that befits a historical monarch. In view of these merits, Mao Tun certainly has good reasons for upholding *The Gall and the Sword* as superior to any other Wu-Yüeh play.

Because of the influence of Communist ideology, however, *The Gall and the Sword* has a weakness which seems inevitable and insurmountable. Generally speaking, characterization in *The Gall and the Sword* is dichotomized along political and class lines. Those on the Wu side are branded as aggressors and assigned unpleasant traits, such as arrogance in Wu Tzu-hsü and greediness in Po-hsi. Those on the Yüeh side, in sharp contrast, are assigned attractive virtues, such as loyalty and statesmanship in Fan-li, and tenacity, self-sacrificial spirit, and charisma in the proletarian hero K'u-ch'eng. I-kao, a Yüeh official, seems to have broken the pattern and acquired unsympathetic traits, but this is explained by his tendency to appease and compromise with the aggressors. King Kou-chien is overshadowed by his eminent subjects, because, leader of the resisters though he is, he nevertheless is a feudalistic ruler.

Whether the characters are villainous aggressors or admirable resisters, they are static in the sense that their fundamental moral natures remain unchanged throughout the dramatic action. Among the dramatis personae, the only character who undergoes some perceivable change in disposition is Kou-chien, but this change is exclusively temperamental, not ethical. His basic commitment to avenge himself and liberate his people is made in the exposition and undergoes no fluctuation thereafter; he displays practically no other concern than the fulfillment of the commitment. His emotional range is extremely narrow: doubts and frustration rarely assail him; smiles hardly ever appear on his careworn face; sorrow over the death or suffering of his subjects is usually the forerunner of fury and determination for revenge, rather than excruciating feeling of helpless anguish. A revealing instance occurs when he is forced to deliver his daughter to Wu as a hostage; he is so angry that the jade tablet held in his hand is squeezed into fragments. But he submits nevertheless to the demand, explaining his motivation to his consort as follows:

When the skin is nonexistent, to what will the hair be attached? Not that I do not have parental love. For twenty years, we have endured enough insult and ill treatment. Madame, which of our

people has not suffered the bereavement of death or the sorrow of
separation from loved ones? Today the ordeal has finally befallen
our royal house. But for the military opportunity and for destroying
Wu at one blow, we must endure the pain. My child, you should
realize the gist of the matter.   (p. 109)

In a discussion of the play by a panel of writers and critics
in Peking, more than one speaker pointed out that Kou-chien
is not affable and can hardly engage the audience's affection.
One critic compares the king with Tseng Wen-ch'ing, a leading
character in *Peking Man*, written during the pre-Communist
era: "The playwright has pointed out many of his weaknesses
and given him much criticism, but the audience infallibly
sympathizes with him. Why? The secret is to be found in the
sympathy and deep affection its author bears for him. The
situation with King Kou-chien in the present play is different:
the author has kept a distance between himself and the character he created."[12] The speaker attributes the saturnine nature
of King Kou-chien largely to the author's inexperience in treating
historical figures according to Communist ideology. The speaker
has overlooked a self-contradictory demand imposed by Communist ideology: as leader of the resisters, King Kou-chien
should be admirable and heroic; but as a ruling monarch,
he cannot be.

It has been noted that depth of thought, embodied in pregnant and precise language, is a major attraction of *The Gall
and the Sword*. But it should also be noted that this depth of
thought is almost exclusively concerned with the feasibility
and desirability of policies and strategies. In other words, it is
a kind of practical widsom, showing little insight into human
psychology or any trace of disinterested ethical deliberation.
As a vehicle for the expression of such wisdom, the language is
suitably precise and graceful but also markedly colorless and
subdued in sentiment. To use Longinus' conception, the language
is not sublime or elevated. Longinus writes: "For the effect
of elevated language is not to persuade the hearers, but to
entrance them."[13] Yet to persuade is precisely the purpose of
The Gall and the Sword, as judged from the circumstances in
which it was written and its prevailing themes, both of which
reflect the concern of a country struggling for economic progress
and political security.

CHAPTER 12

Conclusion

THE commercial and critical success of his plays amply support Ts'ao Yü's reputation as the best writer of Chinese "spoken drama." Most of his major works have gained instantaneous popularity; some still strongly appeal to audiences both in and outside of China. This popular success is significant not only in relation to the playwright himself, but because of its influence on the theater. "On the strength of this success," C. T. Hsia has observed, "a few theatrical companies were established and many other authors turned to playwriting. Without this burgeoning interest the wartime public, in the interior as well as in occupied Shanghai, could not have responded so readily and favorably to the modern theater."[1]

Many other literary historians have also recognized Ts'ao Yü's achievement. Referring to his major pre-Communist works, Wu-chi Liu has written: "Together with *Thunder and Rain* [*Thunderstorm*] these five plays firmly established Ts'ao Yü as the foremost dramatist of modern China, and he was to tower above his predecessors and contemporaries in popularity and literary attainment."[2] "In my opinion," Faubion Bowers has categorically declared, "the greatest of all the playwrights China has produced in modern theatre is Ts'ao Yü."[3] Although his summary comments on Ts'ao Yü's works may be questioned, Jean Monsterleet nevertheless furnishes evidence of Ts'ao Yü's international fame:

Ts'auyu n'atteint pas cet idéal, mais présente un grand nombre de qualités rarement réunies: originalité et adroite adaptation des sources, perfection et variété de la technique, choix personnel de thèmes passionnants, art de conduire l'action et de faire vivre les personnages, émotion communicative qui emporte l'adhésion du spectateur, poésie qui sourd de-ci de-là et détend, langue savoureuse et particulièrement adaptée au dialogue, tout cet ensemble classe Ts'auyu hors pair parmi les dramaturges chinois contemporains.[4]

136

Although Communist literary historians have disapproved of many of Ts'ao Yü's ideas, they pay tribute to his skill and credit him with having raised the artistic standards of contemporary playwrights. A typical statement is made by Ting I: "As a critical, realistic writer Ts'ao Yü is probably one of the best playwrights in the history of modern Chinese literature."[5] Wang Yao, another Communist literary historian, not only concurs with Ting I, but further explains: "He has absorbed techniques of the modern Western theatre and used them to depict Chinese social life. In general, he has elevated the artistic standards of drama: these are his major contributions."[6]

In the judgment of comparative scholars, ingenious and adroit as he is, Ts'ao Yü is nevertheless heavily influenced by and deeply indebted to his great predecessors in the Western theater, particularly Ibsen, O'Neill and Chekhov. "An author may be considered to have been influenced by a foreign author," J. T. Shaw has written on the subject of literary indebtedness, "when something from without can be demonstrated to have produced upon him and/or his artistic works an effect his native literary tradition and personal development do not explain."[7] Since "spoken drama" is based on modern Western theater, no further proof seems needed to demonstrate that Ts'ao Yü is indebted to Western drama for his modes of expression and techniques of composition.

Related to the question of literary influence is that of Ts'ao Yü's originality, about which there has been a long controversy between Ts'ao Yü and his critics. On the surface, the quarrel seems to be a head-on collision; underneath, however, the author and his critics are really arguing different points. On the one hand, Ts'ao Yü denies that he has consciously imitated any author but concedes that perhaps unconsciously he has done so.[8] On the other hand, his critics extend the definition of literary influence to include "unconscious importation of exotic elements into a literary work" and then quote Ts'ao Yü to prove that he is indeed "like an ingrate of a servant, who has stolen threads and threads of golden yarn from the master's house."[9] On another occasion, Ts'ao Yü defends his use of the divided stage in *Sunrise* by pointing out that bawdy-houses customarily pull a curtain to divide the room when necessary and that he knows this device has been successfully employed by O'Neill in

Dynamo.[10] While Ts'ao Yü seems to be merely pointing out a literary parallel, his critics use it to prove that he is now consciously imitating O'Neill.[11] For lack of mutually agreed-on definitions of terms and methodology, this argument could continue indefinitely without reaching any satisfactory conclusion.

Two statements, however, can be cited to clarify the thorny problem of literary indebtedness and originality. "What genuinely moves the reader aesthetically and produces an independent artistic effect has artistic originality, whatever its debts."[12] In light of this definition, the following statement becomes more significant: "While much has been made of Ts'ao Yü's indebtedness to Western dramatists such as Ibsen, Chekhov, and O'Neill, the themes and characters of his plays are much more deeply embedded in the Chinese tradition than those of his predecessors. It was for the originality of his creations and for the local color of his dialogue and characters that the Chinese people preferred Ts'ao Yü's plays to adaptations from and imitations of foreign models."[13]

Ts'ao Yü himself has commented: "It should be the purpose of the Chinese theater . . . to reflect the life and thought patterns of the Chinese people in the tumultuous age of cultural reevaluation."[14] This self-imposed mission, in light of the life and thought patterns of the Chinese people during the period of his most productive years, explains to a large extent not only why Ts'ao Yü has written and developed as he has; it explains also the essential difference between the modern Chinese theater and its counterpart in the West. By extension, it also sheds light on modern Chinese literature in general and establishes that Ts'ao Yü has been in the mainstream of his age.

Since China's earliest military contact with the Western world (in the Opium War, 1839-1842), the primary concern of the nation has been survival, self-strengthening, and recovery of national prestige. International defeat and humiliation not only enhanced domestic crises; they also exposed the fundamental weaknesses of the traditional cultural, social, and political institutions. In search for means to solve external and internal problems, China's intellectual and cultural leaders have suggested various doctrines, philosophies, political and literary forms. In 1919, for example, Ch'en Tu-hsiu, later founder of the Chinese Communist Party, introduced "Mr. Democracy" and

"Mr. Science" as figures capable of solving all problems.[15] Ch'en declared his conscience to be clear when his magazine, *New Youth*, was accused of attacking traditional values through his two invented personages:

They accused this magazine on the grounds that it intended to destroy Confucianism, the code of rituals, the "national quintessence," chastity of women, traditional ethics (loyalty, filial piety, and chastity), traditional arts (the Chinese opera), traditional religion (ghosts and gods), and ancient literature, as well as old-fashioned politics (privileges and government by men alone).[16]

It was for the destruction of traditional ideas and institutions and for the advocacy of new ones (such as democracy and the scientific outlook) that *New Youth* and other magazines were founded and that "spoken drama" was introduced. It is for these same reasons that Ts'ao Yü has written. Thus, while the evils of industrialization were arousing concern in the Western world, the development of industry was one of the most pressing problems for China, a problem to which Ts'ao Yü has addressed himself in *The Bridge*. Similarly, while in the West the growing rejection of many traditional beliefs (such as the attack on Christianity exemplified by Nietzsche's declaration that God is dead) was creating a deep spiritual crisis, China was trying to eliminate the residue of traditional beliefs and systems based on Confucianism. Thus, the basic problems faced by the Chinese dramatists and their contemporary Western counterparts are poles apart. This difference affects not only the choice of subjects for dramatic treatment but the very treatment itself. Since the dramatic treatment of China's problems in the twentieth century is most compatible with realism and naturalism, these styles have prevailed in the modern Chinese theater and in Ts'ao Yü's works. In sharp contrast, a quick succession of divergent styles (such as Impressionism, Expressionism, Surrealism, and Absurdism) has characterized the Western theater.

In *The Wild*, Ts'ao Yü, in order to externalize the inner conflicts and primordial fear of the protagonist, used expressionistic techniques similar to those found in works by Georg Kaiser and Eugene O'Neill. In *Family*, Ts'ao Yü uses asides in an otherwise realistic play. Such devices are rare in Ts'ao Yü's dramas, for with the exception of subtly used symbols, Ts'ao Yü rarely goes beyond realism. Experimentation with styles as ends in themselves is foreign to his method.

Just as he is consistent stylistically, Ts'ao Yü has also dealt in his full-length plays (with the possible exception of *Thunderstorm* and *The Gall and the Sword*), with one basic theme: the need for change. Only the aspects of society being criticized and the recommendations for effectuating changes vary from one play to another. Any shift of focus generally coincides with changes in the national life or in Ts'ao Yü's own situation. Accordingly, Ts'ao Yü's dramatic works can be divided into three groups: his early plays (*Thunderstorm, Sunrise,* and *The Wild*); plays written during World War II and shortly afterward (*Just Thinking, Metamorphosis, Peking Man, Family,* and *The Bridge*); and plays written during the Communist era (*Bright Skies* and *The Gall and the Sword*).

Thematically, the three plays of the first period are so closely related that one critic has regarded them as a trilogy:

Designed as a series by the author, they carry one message, and that is the imminent dissolution of the old order in China. They are harmonious in making a social protest against the existing authority. Their themes, however, differ from one another; *Thunderstorm* points out the deterioration of the old-fashioned family as a traditional social institution; *Sunrise* attacks a sinking society built upon the sandy foundation of deceit, corruption, and tyranny; and *The Wild* treats problems of complex human relations such as love and hatred, gratitude and vengeance, and man's unprotected position in nature. To sum up, Ts'ao Yü in his trilogy wages war against the whole system of feudalism, its morals and its powers, on the strength of his full-fledged new dramatic art.[17]

In order to visualize better Ts'ao Yü's development as a playwright, however, this summary needs further exploration. Ts'ao Yü began to write when he was still a university student, and his first work, *Thunderstorm*, is in some respects that of a poet in his ivory tower. According to Ts'ao Yü himself, writing *Thunderstorm* was emotionally necessary, for he needed some way to discharge the melancholy he felt over "cosmic cruelty," a melancholy which was intensified even further by the traditional Chinese family system. Thus, the play indicts Chou P'u-yüan, the patriarch of a family, for his arrogance and hypocrisy. Yet, Ts'ao Yü is obviously preoccupied above all with the fundamental question of human fate; even though the Chinese family system is attacked, the dramatic structure and the symbols serve more than anything else to underscore the uncertainty of human life. Furthermore, in the Prologue and the Epilogue, religious faith and other-worldliness become the dominant motifs, further eroding the theme of revolt against a social institution.

After his graduation from the University, Ts'ao Yü came into closer contact with existing conditions of Chinese society. The widespread social injustice and suffering which he witnessed had virtually a traumatic effect on him. Thus, in the next two plays, he reacted strongly by advocating the overthrow of the existing order, through violent means if necessary. The alternative is proclaimed in *Sunrise* as one in which God's way will prevail and in *The Wild* as a region where the ground is paved with gold and where men treat each other as brothers. The leftist viewpoint is so obvious that one critic has observed: "Only the most rigorous Marxist critic could disapprove."[18]

For conveying these different messages, the three plays employ different techniques. *Thunderstorm*, along with the forward movement of events, has a backward movement which progresses until sins committed nearly thirty years ago are fully exposed. Since these sins are past events and are thus irreparable, the characters are nearly helpless to avert the impending catastrophe. The structure thus underlines the vulnerability of human beings and the retributive nature of the force which eventually destroys the Chou family. As in *Œdipus Rex* and *Ghosts*, forward and backward movements are closely entwined; furthermore, the play's structural unity is achieved in three ways, through plot, character, and thought.

Sunrise, on the other hand, consists of a series of seemingly disjunctive events which are unified primarily by thought: evil is exposed on every level of society and the need for reform is thus demonstrated. *The Wild* presents yet another interesting variation in techniques; in order to externalize the primordial fear and inner conflict of the protagonist, a series of episodes are presented in an expressionistic style like that used by O'Neill in *The Emperor Jones*.

In *Thunderstorm*, all of the characters are victims. In *Sunrise* and *The Wild*, however, a double ending is used to mete out punishments and rewards. In *Sunrise*, Ch'en Pai-lu, because of

her pessimism and refusal to fight against the dark forces in
society, is shown dying, while Fang Ta-sheng, resolved to deal
with these forces, is shown to have a bright future. Likewise, in
The Wild, though its protagonist is destroyed because of qualms
over the violent means he has used to avenge himself and his
relatives, his loved one, Chin Tzu, is shown on her way to the
ideal region. Quite obviously, this double ending is constructed
to encourage social rebellion and revolution. Unlike *Thunderstorm, Sunrise* and *The Wild* are dialectical in method—they set
up contrasts and lead the characters and the audience to compare
two views and to reach conclusions.

In all these plays, symbols are artistically selected and integrated with the dramatic action to advance the central ideas,
to create appropriate atmosphere, or to augment thematic implications. Some symbols appear in the titles of the plays: the
thunderstorm of *Thunderstorm* suggests the sudden burst of
human passion which overwhelms human reason and underscores
the theme that men are not the masters of their fates. The title
of *Sunrise* indicates the imminent arrival of dawn which will
terminate the reign of darkness. Likewise, the title of *The Wild*
on the realistic level refers to the wilderness where the dramatic
action takes place, but on the symbolical level it signifies the
fear and confusion of the protagonist, who is haunted by a series
of hallucinations.

Other symbols in these plays not only function similarly, but
in some instances combine with those symbols to form a synthesis. For example, the wilderness in *The Wild* is connected
with Ch'ou Hu's ideal world by a railroad, but he cannot find
his way to the railroad station until he has resolved that he
has the right to revenge himself and his oppressed relatives
through violent means. The synthesis reached in the conclusion
suggests that only through the forceful overthrow of the oppressors can people reach the Utopia where men treat one
another as brothers and are free from material needs. Likewise,
the high voltage electric wire which causes the deaths of two
innocent characters in *Thunderstorm* represents the omnipresence
of the indiscriminately destructive force in the universe. A last
example can be drawn from the recurrent songs of the workers
in the background of *Sunrise.* Since these workers regularly
set out for work at daybreak, in sharp contrast to the decadent
wealthy people who do not start their lascivious activities till

sunset, sunrise is obviously connected with the workers, the hope for a just and happy society.

In his recent book, *The Theatre of Revolt*, Robert Brustein has stated that all great modern playwrights from Ibsen to Genet share one common denominator: revolt.[19] Brustein further classifies this revolt into three categories: messianic, in which the dramatist rebels against God and tries to take his place; social, in which the dramatist rebels against the conventions, morals, and values of his society; and existential, in which the dramatist doubts the very value and meaning of human existence. Ts'ao Yü's plays in the first period categorize him as a playwright of social revolt, for they indict certain social institutions. Yet, since the solutions that they advocate transcend any particular society, Ts'ao Yü might also be considered a revolutionary in the messianic sense: *Thunderstorm* protests against cosmic cruelty, *Sunrise* advocate's God's way, and *The Wild* repudiates the verdict of Yama, god of the underworld.

Ts'ao Yü's plays in the second period are far less belligerent. If the early works are those of an angry young man, the middle works are those of a more mature and more temperate writer. Aside from age, it is hard to pin down other causes that explain the transition. One possible cause is Japan's full-scale aggression against China, an event that made national survival rather than domestic reform the primary concern for many Chinese intellectuals. For another, Ts'ao Yü, dissatisfied with his early works, had expressed, in the Postscript to *Sunrise*, great admiration for Chekhov's later plays, and Chekhov is the most temperate among modern dramatists. A less ascertainable but perhaps more profound reason lies in Chinese culture and social conditions. Although Ts'ao Yü continues to stress the necessity for change, his plays bear witness that he has now realized that tradition is not devoid of worth and that modernization does not inevitably require virulent revolt. For all of these possible reasons, Ts'ao Yü's works during this period demonstrate a noticeable change in tone and attitude.

The play that signals the transition is *Just Thinking*, the short farce based on *The Red Velvet Goat* by Josephina Niggli. The play is the most light-hearted among Ts'ao Yü's works, demonstrating that he not only has a sanguine side, but also that he was not always serious. Yet, even in this most carefree production, the author seems to be pondering on the validity of his art and judgment. Through it, Ts'ao Yü seems to be gaining intellectual perspective through self-doubt.

The next four plays, set against backgrounds that extend from Peking to Chengtu and from the late 1920s to the middle 1940s, stress the same theme: in order to survive and prosper, the nation, society, and the individual must undergo drastic changes. *Metamorphosis* shows how a wartime hospital functions effectively after it has been reformed and its new administrators have acquired initiative. *The Bridge*, on the other hand, shows how a wartime steel company, because of harmful government policy and the lack of industrial spirit on the part of its director, falls into ever-increasing financial crisis. Each play includes a group of capable and devoted physicians or engineers, such as Dr. Ting and Dr. Shen Ch'eng-ts'an, and their enthusiasm and dedication are exalting and elevating. But the plays' political implications are obvious: under enlightened leadership, the hospital, the steel company, and, by extension, the country, can prosper; otherwise, despite individual skill and dedication, they are doomed to fail.

Like most of the Chinese intellectuals in the first half of the present century, Ts'ao Yü is convinced that the malaise of China is largely institutional. In the Postscript to *Sunrise*, he has written: "Even though the present society is dark, human nature is not necessarily worse than in ancient times and has not become depraved to any perceivable degree. The ultimate source of all malaise is attributable to institutional defects."[20] In *Family*, the archvillain is Feng Lo-shan, who has caused Kao Chüeh-hui's arrest on false charges and his near death, but after escaping from jail, Kao Chüeh-hui says: "Now I don't hate him that much any more. In the past several days I began to realize that my enemy is not one Feng Lo-shan, but the institution that he represents."[21]

Although his diagnosis of the malaise of Chinese society remains consistent after *Sunrise*, Ts'ao Yü in his early plays seems quite vague about institutional defects. *Sunrise* and *The Wild* attack the plutocratic society and oppressive law but the real villains in those plays are either invisible or dead. Consequently, he chooses to place intense sufferings in the foreground and to relegate the agents of evil to the background. But in *Metamorphosis* and *The Bridge*, the central government, as personified by Inspector Liang and the Director of the Board of Trustees, Ho Hsiang-ju, is held responsible for the success or failure of restructuring and modernizing China. Ts'ao Yü here seems to accept Aristotle's statement in *Politics* that the state is the highest form of community and aims at the highest good. In the final play of the middle period, *The Bridge*, Ts'ao Yü implies that the central government has faltered in its responsibility. The message is obvious.

This message is symbolized, as in the earlier plays, in the title: bridge construction, after the government has arbitrarily canceled its railroad construction contract, will expectedly tide the steel company over its financial crisis until a more enlightened government has been installed. Similarly, the title of *Metamorphosis* indicates the metamorphic changes that China has to undertake in order to renovate and rejuvenate itself. Although written in a realistic style, similar to that used in the earlier works, both plays have minor technical defects, resulting mainly from Ts'ao Yü's anxiety to convince his audience of the validity of his idas. While *The Bridge* has never been popular, *Metamorphosis*, because of its fine characterization and powerful dialogue, has been very successful on the stage and still proves stimulating as a work to be read.

In the other two plays of this period, *Peking Man* and *Family*, Ts'ao Yü studies the hierarchical Chinese family system. Such a system, in which the adult children still live with their parents and the patriarch holds indisputable authority, is a residue of traditional Chinese culture. In the past, such a system provided security and identity for its members, but under the impact of new ideological, commercial, and industrial challenges, such an institution has become increasingly unworkable. Changes are assuredly in order, but unfortunately many members of the family shown in Ts'ao Yü's plays, while basically virtuous, have failed to make the necessary adjustments. Tseng Wen-ch'ing, the protagonist in *Peking Man*, is so used to the idle but esthetic life of the intelligentsia that he is helpless in practical daily life. Domestic frustrations drive him to drug addiction; and, finally, his unrequited love and ignominious return home induce him to commit suicide. Similarly, his counterpart in *Family*, Kao Chüeh-hsin, loses his girl friend and then his wife because of his weak will and compliant attitude.

Thus, *Peking Man* and *Family* are tragedies of maladjustment, frustration, inertia, and nostalgia. Though Ts'ao Yü has not depicted his characters as praiseworthy, he has nevertheless treated them with understanding and leniency. He has even given many sympathetic traits to the patriarchs of these two households, Master Kao and Master Tseng, unlike their counterpart in *Thunderstorm*.

In structure, too, these plays are remarkably different from that of Ts'ao Yü's first play. While *Thunderstorm* progresses toward its catastrophic ending in a rapidly accelerating tempo, the last two plays of the middle period unfold in a seemingly aimless and meandering manner, resembling the idle daily life of the characters. In other words, the microcosmic world in *Thunderstorm* is rapidly changing, bringing to light hidden human relationships and causing catastrophic reversals. In *Peking Man* and *Family*, the leading characters suffer because of stagnancy in their life and inertia of will. In *Thunderstorm*, furthermore, the characters are destroyed because of what they have done, while in the two later plays, the characters merely pine away because they cannot act energetically and effectively.

Despite these dissimilarities, many of the techniques used by Ts'ao Yü in earlier plays not only appear in *Peking Man* and *Family*, but gain subtlety. Most noticeable of these techniques are the double ending and the way in which the symbols are used. At the end of *Peking Man* and *Family*, while the major characters suffer death or bereavement, another group of characters, such as Ssu-fang and Kao Chüeh-hui, in order to seek their own freedom and happiness and to create a better environment for all people, desert their families. In *Peking Man*, Ssu-fang is associated with the pigeon which escapes the cage and flies away, braving storms and defying vultures. Tseng Wen-ch'ing, on the other hand, is compared to the pigeon who is too tame to fly any more. More strikingly, the symbol associated with Master Tseng is a coffin, an object of apathy and death. Ts'ao Yü has indeed become more temperate than before, but there is no ambivalence in his emotion or ambiguity in his conviction about the necessity for change.

It is sometimes asserted that Chekhov's works anticipated the Communist revolution in Russia; the same assertion could also be made of Ts'ao Yü's plays. As noted earlier, it is largely through advocacy of change by writers that the Chinese Communists have gained wide support from intellectuals and students. As the most popular playwright in China, Ts'ao Yü's influence is inestimable. Thus, it is ironical that after the Communists gained control these liberal and humanitarian writers have been reduced to servitude. In this connection, Ts'ao Yü's case is one of the most pathetic. Since the Communist takeover in 1949 he has produced only two plays: *Bright Skies* and *The Gall and the Sword*. As argued earlier, these plays are probably involuntary productions; thus, there is considerable uncertainty about the extent to which these works reflect their author's art and thought. In the "old society," Ts'ao Yü told a Communist interviewer in 1955, he used to shut himself in a room while writing plays; but in writing *Bright Skies* he had to consult Party leaders and theoreticians on the thoughts of the characters and ideology of the dramatic conflicts.[22]

Not only has his method of composition undergone tremendous change; the subject matter of his last two plays also differs markedly from that of his early works. Whereas his early plays deal with national and contemporary issues, his last two plays deal with international or historical ones. Though *Bright Skies* is written with the expressed purpose of convincing intellectuals of the necessity for thought reform under Communist Party guidance, two major incidents are used to support the need: one accusing America of conducting germ warfare in Korea, the other accusing an American doctor of having murdered a Chinese patient. *The Gall and the Sword,* on the other hand, dramatizes the wars between the Wu and Yüeh kingdoms in the fifth century B.C. It is the only historical play among Ts'ao Yü's works. As remote as the subject is, the unfolding of events and characterization follow a distinctly Communist ideology, according to which the proletarians play the leading role in the recovery of a defeated kingdom. Furthermore, separated by two and a half millennia, contemporary audiences are supposed to learn from those earlier exemplary proletarians the spirit of sacrifice and industry essential for the construction of a nation.

To a certain extent, these works continue Ts'ao Yü's earlier stress on change and dedication in constructing a new China. But both *Bright Skies* and *The Gall and the Sword* are submissive in their outlook, for the first play eulogizes the "new society" and the second praises the proletariat as the most heroic and noble-minded class. By direct statement or implication, the Communist Party—the party of the proletariat—is upheld as deserving of the allegiance and loyalty of the people. Such an outlook contrasts sharply with the iconoclastic and rebellious attitude that underlies most of Ts'ao Yü's earlier plays.

In length, too, the early plays differ from the last two. While each of the early full-length plays takes up well over two hundred pages in print, the last two require little more than one hundred each. This difference results to a large extent from the starkness of the dialogue and the meagerness with which issues are explored. Dr. Ting in *Metamorphosis* expresses herself at great length, but her counterpart in *Bright Skies*, Dr. Lin, is habitually terse and cryptic. Although these two characters may be extreme examples, and though the early plays freely use powerful stichomythia, as a rule the characters in the early plays talk freely and argue their positions thoroughly, while characters in the last two plays are guarded, reserved, and often seem to be dissembling. In Aristotelian terms, the dialogue and the dramatic action in the early plays are hierarchically and causally related—statements are maximized or minimized until emotions are aroused and actions are taken. In Ts'ao Yü's last two plays, the speeches appear muffled, as in Dr. Lin's lamentation: "Perhaps I am really getting old."[23] In the last plays, the dialogue at its best attains the status of epigram, as in Wu Tzu-hsü's foreboding over the release of the captured king of Yüeh: "Auspice and portent, blessing and disaster are cognate. Auspice is often the beginning of portent, while a blessing frequently entails disasters."[24] But the dialogue of *Bright Skies* and *The Gall and the Sword* seldom arouses compassion or generates conviction.

The cryptic nature of the dialogue probably indicates its author's caution. Ts'ao Yü himself is extremely apologetic about his deficiency in Communist ideology. His Communist critics, at the very moment they praise his artistic achievement, accuse him of keeping a distance between himself and his characters.[25] In other words, the playwright himself does not profess to understand the ideas in his works, while his critics suspect that he is indifferent to the characters that he creates. All these enhance the probability that the last two plays have been produced as assignments.

Thus, from writing *Thunderstorm* out of emotional necessity,

Ts'ao Yü has come to writing plays out of political necessity. Beginning as a rebel against traditional Chinese culture and existing political and social institutions, Ts'ao Yü has seen the objects of his attack swept away, but in turn he himself has been forced to serve the new order even though it violates the humanitarian ideals that he so ardently depicted in his pre-Communist works.

Although his latest play, *The Gall and the Sword*, reveals that his powers are undiminished, Ts'ao Yü's fame rests primarily on his pre-Communist works. As critics and literary historians have amply testified, Ts'ao Yü's position in modern Chinese literature is assured. As interest in China grows in the Western world, he may gain even more international attention and may yet come to share the fame of the great Western dramatists.

Notes and References

Preface

1. For representative views by historians, see the concluding chapter.

2. Typical of such studies are:

Ting I, "Dramatic Works of Hung Sheng and Ts'ao Yü," *A Short History of Modern Chinese Literature* (Peking, 1957), pp. 279-86, or pp. 180-84 in the English translation (Peking, 1959), where the author's name is romanized as Ting Yi.

Wang Yao, *A Draft History of Modern Chinese Literature* (Shanghai, 1953), pp. 271-75 in Vol. I, and pp. 154-58 in Vol. II.

3. For example, see Ting Miao, *Chinese Communist Drama of the Coalition Period* (Hong Kong, 1954), pp. 18-30, 61-77.

4. For a list of some of these studies, see the Bibliography under David Y. Chen and Joseph Shiu-ming Lau.

Chapter One

1. T'ien Han and others, ed., *Source Materials on Fifty Years of Chinese Spoken Drama*, I (Peking, 1958), 17-19.

2. *Ibid.*, I, 17-18.

3. *Ibid.*, I, 31.

4. Ou-yang Yü-ch'ien, "Spoken Drama, New Opera, and the Tradition of Chinese Theatre Arts," *Literary Gazette*, XV (1959), 3.

5. Wu-chi Liu, "Book the Ninth, the Modern Period (A.D. 1900-1950)," *A History of Chinese Literature*, by Herbert A. Giles (New York, 1967), p. 476; Hong Kong Wen-hsueh Yen-chiu-she, ed., *A Comprehensive Anthology of Modern Chinese Literature: 1928-38* (Hong Kong, 1968), I, 24; Yao Hsin-nung, "Drama Chronicle," *T'ien Hsia Monthly*, III (August, 1936), 45, 49.

6. Chao Chia-pi, ed., *A Comprehensive Anthology of Modern Chinese Literature: 1917-27* (Hong Kong, 1962), X, 136.

7. *Ibid.*, IX, 26-28.

8. Fu Ssu-nien, "Further Discussion on Drama Reform," *New Youth Monthly*, V (October, 1918), 349-50, 355-56.

9. Chao Chia-pi, IX, 29.

10. T'ien Ch'in, *The Chinese Drama Movement* (Shanghai, 1946), pp. 105-07.

11. Chao Chia-pi, IX, 32.

12. T'ien Han, I, 19.

13. "Correct Understanding and Application of the Stanislavsky Performing System," *Literary Gazette*, II (1953), 35-36.

14. Chao Chia-pi, IX, 66-67.

15. T'ien Han, I, 110-11; Chao Chia-pi, IX, 71.

16. Chao Chia-pi, IX, 33-35. For an interesting analysis of Chinese audience preference of Ibsen to Shaw, see Hsiao Ch'ien, "Ibsen in China (and the Chinese Annoyance at Bernard Shaw)," *The Dragon Beards Versus the Blueprints* (London, 1944), pp. 16-20.

17. T'ien Han is another modern Chinese playwright who has gained international attention. Recent studies on him include:

Constantine Tung, "T'ien Han and the Romantic Ibsen," *Modern Drama*, IX (1967), 389-95;

Constantine Tung, "Lonely Search into the Unknown: T'ien Han's Early Plays," *Comparative Drama*, II (1968), 44-54.

18. Ting Yi, *A Short History of Modern Chinese Literature* (Peking, 1959), p. 146.

19. For a comparative study of these three plays, see David Y. Chen, "Two Chinese Adaptations of Eugene O'Neill's *The Emperor Jones*," *Modern Drama*, IX (February, 1967), 431-39. Though concerned primarily with the issue of literary influence, Dr. Chen has many penetrating observations on *The Wild*. His analysis of the use of symbols in *The Wild* is particularly interesting.

20. Kai-yu Hsu, trans. and ed., *Twentieth Century Chinese Poetry* (Garden City, N.Y., 1963), p. xxi.

21. C. T. Hsia, *A History of Modern Chinese Fiction* (New Haven: Yale University Press, 1961), p. 21.

22. Three different years have been given for Ts'ao Yü's birth: 1905 (in relatively early publications such as *1500 Modern Chinese Novels and Plays,* ed. Joseph Schynes), 1909 (on catalog cards in many U.S. libraries), and 1910 (in publications from Peking since 1949). Prof. Ping-ying Hsien, writer and critic, and a close friend of Ts'ao Yü, once told me that Ts'ao Yü might have back-dated his own birth following the unprecedented success of *Thunderstorm* (1934) in order to make people believe that he was older than he actually was (most American writers today would probably tend to do just the opposite).

His birthplace is also uncertain. Though Chienkiang, Hupei, has been generally accepted as his "native place," it may just be a place where his ancestors once lived, not the place where he was actually born. While at the present time I cannot ascertain what's what, Ts'ao Yü definitely grew up (from no later than his fourth year) in Tientsin, Hopei, a metropolis of North China (in contrast to Chienkiang, a small town in Central China), where his father had a large house in the foreign compound.

23. Ts'ao Yü, "Preface," *Thunderstorm* (Shanghai, 1936), p. iii. A full English rendering of the Preface can be found in *T'ien Hsia Monthly*, III (1936), 270-83.

24. The course of Ts'ao Yü's life during this period is hard to trace. While teaching at the women's college, he seems to have taken graduate work at Tsing Hua University, though nothing more about it has come to light thus far. Furthermore, as the Sino-Japanese War was approaching, the National Academy of Dramatic Arts was moved to the interior cities including Chungking. Though Ts'ao Yü was known to have been for a time the principal of the Academy during wartime, the date when his position terminated cannot be ascertained at the present time.

25. Ts'ao Yü, "Postscript," *Sunrise*, 26th ed. (Shanghai, 1946), p. 1.

26. *Ibid.*, pp. 2-3.

27. Ting Yi, p. 180.

28. See John Milton, "Areopagitica," *The Complete Works of John Milton*, IV (New York, 1931), 346.

29. Liu, "Book the Ninth," p. 479.

30. Chi-hua Ch'eng and others, *A History of the Development of the Chinese Moving Picture*, Vol. II (Peking, 1963), 265.

31. "Ts'ao Yü," *Who Is Who in Communist China* (Hong Kong: Union Research Institute, 1966).

32. Liu, "Book the Ninth," p. 477; "Ts'ao Yü on the Creation of *Bright Skies*," *Literary Gazette*, XVII (1955), 19.

33. *Jen-min Jih-pao*, May 24, 1952.

34. Since the Communist takeover, practically all of Ts'ao Yü's discussions of his early plays contain some self-disparaging criticism. For a list of such discussions, see Bibliography. See also prefaces to his works republished by the Communists.

35. Ting Yi, pp. 181-82.

36. Ts'ao Yü, "Support the Constitutional Draft of the People's Republic of China," *Literary Gazette*, XIV (1954), 7.

37. Ts'ao Yü, "We Must Reduce Royalty," *Literary Gazette*, XIX (1958), 18.

38. For further details, see Hsia, pp. 336-38.

39. Ts'ao Yü, "On What Road Did Hu Feng Walk?" *Literary Gazette*, IX and X (1955), 38.

40. *Ibid.*

41. In 1963, Ts'ao Yü was reportedly writing a historical play on the subject of Wang Chao-chun, but there is no confirmation that the play has been published or even written. A pathetic beauty of the Han Dynasty, Wang Chao-chun has been treated in Yüan Drama, K'un-ch'u, Peking Opera, and spoken drama (for example, in Kuo

Mo-jo's *Trilogy of Three Revolutionary Women*). It will be interesting to see how Ts'ao Yü will treat such a popular historical figure;
even his reported attempt to write on Wang Chao-chun is significant,
for it indicates Ts'ao Yü's aversion to dealing with contemporary
subjects.

42. D. W. Fokkema, *Literary Doctrine in China and Soviet Influence, 1956-1960* (The Hague, 1965), pp. 67-70.

43. "Ts'ao Yü on the Creation of *Bright Skies*," *Literary Gazette*,
XVII (1955), 22.

44. "In Hope of More Good Works to Come—Writers' Panel
Discussion on Great Leap Forward in Literature," *People's Literature*,
CI (April, 1958), 3.

45. Mao Tse-tung, *On Art and Literature* (Peking, 1966), p. 104.

46. Hsia, p. 94.

Chapter Two

1. Ts'ao Chü-jen, *New Words on Men and Matters* (Hong Kong,
1963), p. 264.

2. "Chinese Plays on the Russian Stage," *Dramatic Gazette*, II
(Jan., 1960), 34-35. The article was prepared by the information
service of the Embassy of the U.S.S.R. in Peking. Since the Sino-
Russian split was then just surfacing, the article was highly laudatory
and even hyperbolic.

3. *On the Art of Poetry*, trans. Ingram Bywater (Oxford, 1959),
p. 53.

4. *Ibid.*, p. 45.

5. *Ibid.*, p. 38.

6. *Ibid.*, p. 60.

7. Ts'ao Yü, "Thunder and Rain," trans. Yao Hsin-nung, *T'ien
Hsia Monthly*, III (1936), 530. This is the authorized translation
appearing in III (1936), 284-295 [Prologue]; 363-411 [Act I];
486-530 [Act II] and IV (1937), 61-95 [Act III]; 176-221 [Act IV
and Epilogue]. The romanization of the characters' names has been
changed in order to conform to the Wade-Giles system.

8. *Greek Tragedy* (New York, n.d.), pp. 134-40.

Chapter Three

1. Ts'ao Yü, "Postscript," *Sunrise*, 26th ed. (Shanghai, 1946), p. 4.

2. *Ibid.*, pp. 8-9. The translation is mine.

3. *Ibid.*

4. The translation used in the text is from Lao Tzu, *The Way
of Life*, trans. R. B. Blakney (New York, 1955), p. 130.

5. See *The Apocalypse*, xxi, 1.

6. The character's name in Chinese is Hsiao tung-hsi (little thing or little creature); The Shrimp is used by A. C. Barnes in his translation of *Sunrise* (Peking, 1960). The first pagination following quoted passages in the text refers to Ts'ao Yü's Chinese version; the second, to Barnes's translation.

7. Ts'ao Yü, p. 220; Barnes, pp. 174-75.

8. Ts'ao Yü, p. 182; Barnes, p. 146.

9. Joseph Shiu-ming Lau, "Ts'ao Yü, the Reluctant Disciple of Chekhov and O'Neill" (unpublished dissertation, Indiana University, 1966), p. 57. Part of this dissertation is published in *Modern Drama*, IX (Feb., 1967), 358-72.

10. Ts'ao Yü, p. 136; Barnes, p. 106.

11. Ts'ao Yü, p. 133; Barnes, p. 102.

12. Ts'ao Yü, p. 13; Barnes, p. 6.

13. Ts'ao Yü, p. 37. This sentence, along with a few others, is omitted from Barnes's translation, probably because it tarnishes the "nobility of the people."

14. Ts'ao Yü, p. 194; Barnes, p. 154.

15. Ts'ao Yü, p. 187; Barnes, p. 150.

16. Ts'ao Yü, p. 235; Barnes, pp. 188-89.

17. Ts'ao Yü, "Postscript," p. 10.

18. Hubert Heffner, *Modern Theater Practice*, 4th ed. (New York, 1959), pp. 61-64; Oscar G. Brockett, *The Theatre: An Introduction* (New York, 1964), p. 251.

19. Donald Clive Stuart, *The Development of Dramatic Art* (New York, 1960), pp. 601-2.

20. *Ibid.*, p. 603.

Chapter Four

1. Ts'ao Yü, *The Wild* (Shanghai, 1936), p. 129. The English translations of the script throughout this chapter are mine.

2. David Y. Chen, "Two Chinese Adaptations of Eugene O'Neill's *The Emperor Jones*," *Modern Drama*, IX (February, 1967), 341-39; David Y. Chen, "The Trilogy of Ts'ao Yü and Western Drama," *Asia and the Humanities* (Bloomington, Ind., 1959), ed. Horst Frenz, p. 34. See also Joseph Shiu-ming Lau, "Ts'ao Yü, the Reluctant Disciple of Chekhov and O'Neill (unpublished dissertation, Indiana University, 1966), pp. 81-90.

3. Karl Marx and Friedrich Engels, *The Communist Manifesto*, ed. Samuel H. Beer (New York, 1955), p. 46.

4. Ting I, *A Short History of Modern Chinese Literature*, II (Peking, 1957), 285. The translation is mine.

Chapter Five

1. Josephina Niggli, *Mexican Folk Plays* (Chapel Hill, N. C., 1938), p. xvi.

2. *Ibid.*, p. 120.

3. *Ibid.*, p. 149.

4. *Ibid.*, p. 137.

5. *Ibid.*, p. xi.

6. *Ibid.*, p. xviii.

7. *Ibid.*, p. xi.

8. Ts'ao Yü, *Just Thinking* (Shanghai, 1940), p. 81.

9. *Ibid.*, p. 82.

10. Only after vigorous investigation was I able to locate a copy of the play in the Yale University Library.

11. David Y. Chen, "The Trilogy of Ts'ao Yü and Western Drama," *Asia and the Humanities,* ed. Horst Frenz (Bloomington, Ind., 1959), pp. 26-37.

12. Ts'ao Yü, *Thunderstorm* (Shanghai, n.d.), pp. i-ii. The translation is mine.

13. For example, see A. C. Scott, *Literature and Art in Twentieth Century China* (New York, 1963), p. 43.

14. Ts'ao Yü, "Postscript," *Sunrise,* 26th ed. (Shanghai, 1946), pp. 9-10. The second and third paragraphs in the passage are the translation of David Y. Chen.

15. *Ibid.*, p. 10.

16. Ts'ao Yü not only denies conscious imitation, he disapproves of it; see above, pp. 23-24.

Chapter Six

1. Ts'ao Yü, *Metamorphosis* (Shanghai, 1940), p. 295. The English translations of the text throughout this chapter are mine.

2. Ting Miao, *Chinese Communist Drama of the Coalition Period* (Hong Kong, 1954), p. 71.

3. Quoted by Ting Miao, p. 61.

4. Peng Fei, "The Arts in China Today," *The China Magazine,* XVIII (February, 1948), 39.

5. *Tragedy and the Theory of Drama* (Detroit, 1966), pp. 86-90, 98, 111-12.

6. *A History of Modern Chinese Fiction* (New Haven: Yale University Press, 1961), p. 381.

7. Ting I, *A Short History of Modern Chinese Literature* (Peking, 1957), p. 285.

8. Ting Miao, p. 75.

9. Bertolt Brecht, *The Life of Galileo,* trans. Desmond I. Vesey (London, 1963), p. 108.

10. *Brecht: The Man and His Work* (New York, 1961), p. 67.

11. *The Development of Dramatic Art* (New York, 1960) p. 483.

Chapter Seven

1. Ts'ao Yü, *Peking Man* (Shanghai, 1941), pp. 117-18. The English translations in this chapter are mine.

2. David Y. Chen, *"The Hairy Ape* and *The Peking Man*: Two Types of Primitivism in Modern Society," *Yearbook of Comparative and General Literature,* XV (1966), 214.

3. *Ibid.*

Chapter Eight

1. Wang Yao, *A Draft History of Modern Chinese Literature,* II (Shanghai, 1953), 234. Olga Lang quotes Wang, but mistakes "twenty years old" for "twenty years ago." See Olga Lang, *Pa Chin and His Writings* (Cambridge, Mass., 1967), p. 78.

2. "Best Sellers in Chungking," *China at War,* XII (May, 1944), 15.

3. Ts'ao Yü, *Family* (Shanghai, 1947), p. 28. The English translations from the play in this chapter are mine. Excerpts of the play have been translated and published in "From *Family,* a Play by Ts'ao Yü," *Life and Letters and the London Mercury,* LX (January, 1954), 35-64.

4. Percy Bysshe Shelley, *Ode to the West Wind,* IV, 5-11.

Chapter Nine

1. John Milton, "Areopagitica," *The Complete Works of John Milton,* IV (New York: Columbia University Press, 1931), 346.

2. Ts'ao Yü, *The Bridge* (Hong Kong, 1965?), pp. 122-23. The English translation is mine.

3. First published in *Wen-i Fu-hsing (Literary Renaissance),* a literary monthly, in Shanghai, in 1945, when China's civil war was intense, *The Bridge* attracted little attention and soon became hardly available. No university in the United States is known to have had a copy of the play until Wen-i (Literature and Arts) Press, Hong Kong, reprinted the play from the magazine probably in 1965 or shortly afterwards. (No date of reprinting is given.)

Chapter Ten

1. See Introduction, pp. 24-27.

2. On the basis of the present play, certain critics have concluded that it is hopeless for Ts'ao Yü to regain his former talent and artistry;

see, for example, A. C. Scott, *Literature and the Arts in Twentieth Century China* (Garden City, New York, 1963), pp. 43-44.

3. Ts'ao Yü, *Bright Skies* (Peking, 1956), p. 92. The English translations of passages in this chapter are mine.

Chapter Eleven

1. James Legge, trans. *The Chinese Classics*, II, *The Works of Mencius* (Hong Kong, 1960), 478.

2. T'ien Han, "On the Treatment of Subject Matter," *Literary Gazette*, VII (1961), 6-7.

3. Mao Tun, *On History and Historical Plays* (Peking, 1962), p. 1.

4. *Ibid.*, p. 139.

5. Ts'ao Yü, *The Gall and the Sword* (Peking, 1962), p. 12. The English translations of the text throughout are mine.

6. See "Hsi-shih" under "Hsi" in *Mathews' Chinese-English Dictionary*, rev. American ed.

7. Margaret Webster, *Shakespeare without Tears*, 5th ed. (Greenwich, Conn., 1966), p. 118.

8. "K'u" in *Mathews' Chinese-English Dictionary*.

9. "Ch'eng" in *Mathews' Chinese-English Dictionary*.

10. Ts'ao Yü, p. 107. Apparently, K'u-ch'eng's misleading confession had settled the problem of the missing sword only temporarily, but there is no indication in the script of the continued investigation until this moment.

11. Chang Kuang-nien, "On the Techniques of *The Gall and the Sword*," *Dramatic Gazette*, I (January, 1962), 4.

12. "A Panel Discussion on *The Gall and the Sword* in Correspondence," *Literary Gazette*, I (January, 1962), 16.

13. T. S. Dorsch, *Classical Literary Criticism* (London, 1965), p. 100.

Chapter Twelve

1. C. T. Hsia, *A History of Modern Chinese Fiction: 1917-1957* (New Haven: Yale University Press, 1961), pp. 317-18.

2. Wu-chi Liu, "Book the Ninth, Modern Period," *History of Chinese Literature*, by Herbert A. Giles (New York, 1967), p. 476.

3. Faubion Bowers, *Theatre in the East: A Survey of Asian Dance and Drama* (New York, 1960), p. 299.

4. Jean Monsterleet, *Sommets de la littérature chinoise contemporaine* (Paris, 1953), p. 107.

5. Ting Yi, *A Short History of Modern Chinese Literature* (Peking, 1959), p. 183. "Probably" in the passage in the Chinese version is "chung pu shih wei," which can be better rendered as "nevertheless,"

referring to the historian's reservation about Ts'ao Yü's ideological "weaknesses." See the original text, p. 286.

6. Wang Yao, *A Draft History of Modern Chinese Literature,* II (Shanghai, 1953), 158.

7. J. T. Shaw, "Literary Indebtedness and Comparative Literary Studies," *Comparative Literature: Method and Perspective,* ed. Newton P. Stallknecht and Horst Frenz (Carbondale, 1961), p. 65.

8. See Chapter 5.

9. *Ibid.*

10. Ts'ao Yü, "Postscript," *Sunrise* (Shanghai, 1946), p. 16.

11. David Y. Chen, "The Trilogy of Ts'ao Yü and Western Drama," *Asia and the Humanities* (Bloomington, 1959), ed. Horst Frenz, p. 34.

12. J. T. Shaw, p. 60.

13. Wu-chi Liu, pp. 478-79.

14. For further information, see Chapter 1.

15. Chow Tse-tsung, *The May Fourth Movement* (Stanford, Calif., 1967), p. 59.

16. *Ibid.*

17. David Y. Chen, p. 29.

18. C. T. Hsia, p. 318.

19. Robert Brustein, *The Theatre of Revolt* (Boston, 1964), pp. 3-17.

20. Ts'ao Yü, "Postscript," *Sunrise,* p. 20.

21. Ts'ao Yü, *Family* (Shanghai, n.d.), p. 246.

22. "Ts'ao Yü on the Creation of *Bright Skies,*" *Literary Gazette,* XVII (1955), 19-20. This article is based on an interview with Ts'ao Yü and written by an unspecified staff member of the magazine.

23. Ts'ao Yü, *Bright Skies* (Peking, 1956), p. 71.

24. Ts'ao Yü, *The Gall and the Sword* (Peking, 1962), p. 12.

25. "A Panel Discussion of *The Gall and the Sword* in Correspondence," *Literary Gazette,* I (January, 1962), 17-19.

Selected Bibliography

PRIMARY SOURCES

In Chinese:

Cheng tsai hsiang (*Just Thinking*). Shanghai: Wen-hua sheng-huo ch'u-pan-she, 1940.

Chia (*Family*). 26th ed. Shanghai: Wen-hua sheng-huo ch'u-pan-she, 1947.

Ch'iao (*The Bridge*). Hong Kong: Wen-i shu-chü, 1965?

Jih ch'u (*Sunrise*). 26th ed. Shanghai: Wen-hua sheng-huo ch'u-pan-she, 1946.

Lei yü (*Thunderstorm*). Shanghai: Wen-hua sheng-huo ch'u-pan-she, 1936.

Ming lang ti t'ien (*Bright Skies*). Peking: Jen-min wen-hsüeh ch'u-pan-she, 1956.

Pei-ching jen (*Peking Man*). Shanghai: Wen-hua sheng-huo ch'u-pan-she, 1941.

Shui pien (*Metamorphosis*). Shanghai: Wen-hua sheng-huo ch'u-pan-she, 1940.

Tan chien p'ien (*The Gall and the Sword*). Peking: Chung-kuo hsi-ch'u ch'u-pan-she, 1962.

Ts'ao Yü chü-pen hsüan (*Collected Plays*). Peking: Jen-min wen-hsüeh ch'u-pan-she, 1954.

Ts'ao Yü hsüan chi (*Collected Works*). Rev. ed. Peking: Jen-min wen-hsüeh ch'u-pan-she, 1962.

Yen yang t'ien (*Sunny Sky*). Shanghai: Wen-hua sheng-huo ch'u-pan-she, 1948.

Yüan yeh (*The Wild*). Shanghai: Wen-hua sheng-huo ch'u-pan-she, 1936.

In English:

Bright Skies. Trans. Chang Pei-chi. Peking: Foreign Languages Press, 1960.

Sunrise. Trans. A. C. Barnes. Peking: Foreign Languages Press, 1960.

"Thunder and Rain." Trans. Yao Hsin-nung, *T'ien Hsia Monthly*, III (1936), 284-95, 363-411, 486-530; IV (1937), 61-95, 176-221.

Thunderstorm. Trans. Wang Tso-liang and A. C. Barnes. Peking: Foreign Languages Press, 1958.

SECONDARY SOURCES

In Chinese:

CHAO, CHIA-PI, ed. *Chung-kuo hsin-wen-hsüeh ta-hsi (A Comprehensive Anthology of Modern Chinese Literature: 1917-27)*. 10
vols. Shanghai: Shanghai liang-yu t'u-shu yin-shua kung-shih,
1935-36.

CH'ENG, CHI-HUA, AND OTHERS. *Chung-kuo tien-ying fa-chan shih (A
History of the Development of the Chinese Moving Picture)*. 2
vols. Peking: Chung-kuo tien-ying ch'u-pan-she, 1963.

HONG KONG WEN-HSÜEH YEN-CHIU HUI, ed. *Chung-kuo hsin-wen-
hsüeh ta-hsi hsu pien (A Comprehensive Anthology of Modern
Chinese Literature, 1928-1938)*. 10 vols. Hong Kong, 1968.

HU FENG. *Hu Feng wen chi (Collected Works)*. Shanghai: Ch'un-
ming shu-tien, 1948.

MAO TUN. *(Kuan-yü li-shih ho li-shih chu (About History and Historical Plays)*. Peking: Tso-chia ch'u-pan-she, 1962.

T'IEN, CH'IN. *Chung-kuo hsi-ch'u yün-tung (The Chinese Drama
Movement)*. Shanghai, 1946.

T'IEN, HAN, AND OTHERS, ed. *Chung-kuo hua-ch'u yün-tung wu-shih
nien shih-liao (Source Materials on Fifty Years of Chinese Spoken
Drama)*. 1st vol. Peking: Chung-kuo hsi-ch'u ch'u-pan-she, 1958.

TING, I. *Chung-kuo hsien-tai wen-hsueh shih-lüeh (A Short History
of Modern Chinese Literature)*. Peking: Tso-chia ch'u-pan-she,
1957.

TING, MIAO. *Chung-kung t'ung-chan hsi-ch'u (Chinese Communist
Drama of the Coalition Period)*. Hong Kong: Ya-chou ch'u-
pan-she, 1954.

TS'AO, CHÜ-JEN. *Wen t'an wu-shih nien (Fifty Years of Chinese
Literature)*. 2 vols. Hong Kong: Hsin Wen-hua, 1955.

————. *Jen-shih hsin yü (New Words on Men and Matters)*. Hong
Kong: I-Ch'u ch'u-pan-she, 1963.

WANG, CHE-FU. *Chung-kuo hsin-wen-hsüeh yün-tung shih (A History
of the New Literary Movement in China)*. Hong Kong: Yüan-
tung, 1967.

WANG, YAO. *Chung-kuo hsin-wen-hsüeh shih-kao (A Draft History
of Modern Chinese Literature)*. 2 vols. Shanghai: Hsin-wen-i
ch'u-pan-she, 1953.

In Other Languages:

BOWERS, FAUBION. *Theatre in the East: A Survey of Asian Dance
and Drama*. New York: T. Nelson, 1960.

CHEN, JACK. *The Chinese Theatre*. New York: Roy Publishers, 1948.

CHOW, TSE-TSUNG. *The May Fourth Movement: Intellectual Revolution in Modern China*. Stanford: Stanford University Press, 1967.

GILES, HERBERT ALLEN. *History of Chinese Literature*. With a supplement on the modern period by Wu-chi Liu. New York: F. Ungar, 1967.

HSIA, C. T. *A History of Modern Chinese Fiction, 1917-1957*. New Haven: Yale University Press, 1961.

LAU, JOSEPH SHIU-MING. "Ts'ao Yü, the Reluctant Disciple of Chekhov and O'Neill" (Unpublished doctoral dissertation). Bloomington: Indiana University, 1967. *Ts'ao Yü, the Reluctant Disciple of Chekhov and O'Neill: A Study in Literary Influence*, Hong Kong: University Press, 1970.

MONSTERLEET, JEAN. *Sommets de la littérature chinoise contemporaine*. Paris: Domat, 1953.

SCHYNS, JOSEPH. *1500 Modern Chinese Novels and Plays*. Ridgewood, N.J.: The Gregg Press, 1966.

SCOTT, A. C. *Literature and the Arts in Twentieth Century China*. Garden City, N.Y.: Doubleday, 1963.

TING, YI. *A Short History of Modern Chinese Literature*. Trans. Cheng Hsien-lien and others. Peking: Foreign Languages Press, 1959.

ARTICLES

In Chinese:

"Chinese Plays on the Russian Stage," *Dramatic Gazette* (Hsi-ch'u pao), II (1960), 34-35.

FU SSU-NIEN. "Further Discussion on Drama Reform," *New Youth Monthly* (Hsin ch'ing nien), V (October, 1918), 373-84.

—————. "Various Aspects of Drama Reform," *New Youth Monthly*, V (1918), 345-64.

"In Hope of More Good Works to Come—Writers' Panel Discussion on Great Leap Forward in Literature," *People's Literature* (Jen-min wen-hsüeh), CI (1958), 1-4.

LIU YU-K'UAN. "Rambling on *The Gall and the Sword*," *Dramatic Gazette*, XXI-XXII (1961), 4-10.

OU-YANG YÜ-CH'IEN. "Spoken Drama, New Opera, and the Tradition of Chinese Theatre Arts," *Literary Gazette*, XV (1959), 2-8; XVI (1959), 16-21.

"A Panel Discussion on *The Gall and the Sword* in Correspondence," *Literary Gazette*, I (1962), 9-19.

T'IEN HAN. "On the Treatment of Subject Matter," *Literary Gazette*, VII (1961), 6-7.

"Ts'ao Yü on the Creation of *Bright Skies*," *Literary Gazette*, XVII (1955), 19-22.

TS'AO YÜ. "On What Road Did Hu Feng Walk?" *Literary Gazette*, IX and X (1955), 38-39.

—————. "Rambling on Playwriting," *Dramatic Gazette* (1962), 1-2.

————. "Support the Constitutional Draft of the People's Republic of China," *Literary Gazette*, XIV (1954), 6-7.

————. "We Must Reduce Royalty," *Literary Gazette*, XIX (1958), 18.

————. "We Will Do What Our Enemies Fear Most," *Literary Gazette*, XI (1955), 33-34.

In Other Languages:

"Best Sellers in Chungking," *China at War*, XII (May, 1944), 15-16.

CHEN, DAVID Y. "*The Hairy Ape* and *The Peking Man*: Two Types of Primitivism in Modern Society," *Yearbook of Comparative and General Literature*, XV (1966), 214-20.

————. "The Trilogy of Ts'ao Yü and Western Drama," *Asia and the Humanities*, pp. 26-37. Ed. Horst Frenz. Bloomington: Indiana University Press, 1959.

————. "Two Chinese Adaptations of Eugene O'Neill's *The Emperor Jones*," *Modern Drama*, IX (February 1967), 431-39.

LAU, JOSEPH S. M. "Ts'ao Yü, the Reluctant Disciple of Chekhov: A Comparative Study of *Sunrise* and *The Cherry Orchard*," *Modern Drama*, IX (February, 1967), 358-72.

————. "Two Emancipated Phaedras: Chou Fan-yi and Abbie Putnam as Social Rebels," *The Journal of Asian Studies*, XXV, 4 (August, 1966), 699-711.

MEKADA, MAKOTO. "On Ts'ao Yü's Plays," *Studies in Literature* (Published by Kynshu University), II (1959), 65-97.

MESERVE, WALTER J., AND RUTH I. MESERVE. "Ts'ao Yü: Dramatist in Communist China," *Comparative Drama*, II (1968), 115-21.

"New Play by a Great Dramatist," *China News Analysis*, LXIII (December, 1954), 5-7.

NIKOL, SKAYA L. A., "Dramaturgiya Ts'ao Yü," *Sovetskaya Kitsevederiya*, 73-85.

PENG, FEI. "The Arts in China Today," *The China Magazine*, XVIII (February, 1948), 37-43.

YANG, YU. "The Playwright Ts'ao Yü," *Chinese Literature*, XI (November, 1963), 97-103.

YAO, HSING-NUNG. "Editorial Commentary," *T'ien Hsia Monthly*, III (1936), 211-14.

Index

(The works of Ts'ao Yü are listed under his name)